BEYOND THE LAW OF ATTRACTION

HOW TO WORK WITH THE UNIVERSE FOR A HAPPY AND SUCCESSFUL LIFE JOURNEY

Dr. Elizabeth Conway

BALBOA.
PRESS
A DIVISION OF HAY HOUSE

NKJV: Scripture taken from the New King James Version®. Copyright
© 1982 by Thomas Nelson. Used by permission. All rights reserved.

Balboa Press books may be ordered through booksellers or by contacting:

Balboa Press
A Division of Hay House
1663 Liberty Drive
Bloomington, IN 47403
www.balboapress.com
1 (877) 407-4847

Because of the dynamic nature of the Internet, any web addresses or
links contained in this book may have changed since publication and
may no longer be valid. The views expressed in this work are solely those
of the author and do not necessarily reflect the views of the publisher,
and the publisher hereby disclaims any responsibility for them.

The author of this book does not dispense medical advice or prescribe the use
of any technique as a form of treatment for physical, emotional, or medical
problems without the advice of a physician, either directly or indirectly. The
intent of the author is only to offer information of a general nature to help
you in your quest for emotional and spiritual well-being. In the event you use
any of the information in this book for yourself, which is your constitutional
right, the author and the publisher assume no responsibility for your actions.

Cover art and graphics by Laura Wattie and Georgia Rouette @ Grendesign

Print information available on the last page.

ISBN: 978-1-5043-0707-9 (sc)
ISBN: 978-1-5043-0708-6 (e)

Balboa Press rev. date: 03/27/2017

PREFACE

Beyond the Law of Attraction was first a workshop I wrote because of what I had observed as some people's "missed" interpretation of the law. I found many were judging themselves harshly, believing they had attracted everything that they perceived as negative into their lives. Others were quick to call another into account, asking, "What did you do—and why—to attract that into your life?" I seriously doubt making yourself (or someone else) wrong was the intention of those in the past who wrote about this universal law. And it was not created for that purpose. I call this a missed interpretation or a missed understanding. The time is ripe for the lessons of laws beyond this one law.

I have no need to write this book other than for it to make a difference—a positive difference. If it can make that difference for just one person, and even if that one is only me, my time has been well spent. I seek to look honestly to myself and my motives for writing this book. Is it ego or spirit that is the motivator? Perhaps it is both, yet I know when I am on a roll, there is no sign of ego, just the joy of being the voice of my spirit, a voice needing and wanting to manifest in word for myself and perhaps another, the joy of knowing and being in spirit, living a life in joy rather than pain.

I know that many of you are in pain physically, mentally, and emotionally. You may have serious human health issues; you may have been abused by someone's brutality or left traumatised by a life experience.

I am not here to minimise or trivialise this, or suggest in any way that you attracted that to yourself. In fact, I am here to state those who say this, do so from a lack of understanding of other natural and universal laws in play; these laws impact our lives in many ways. Spirituality for me is not another religion to make you feel bad about yourself. (Not all religions teach judgement and damnation; sometimes, this comes from how the teachings have been interpreted and then reinforced by the self.) I'm aware of the impact certain belief systems can have on people's lives. We are powerful beings because of our creator and our creation (see chapter 7) We can see heaven or hell and make our lives so. There is much evidence all around us, through the lives of others, as to the reality of this. Yet there are also situations out of our control that we are not responsible for; we did not "attracted" them.

I share here what I know: my experiences and how I understand and interpret spirituality, the divine source, and universal laws and principles. I believe these laws and principles have been put into place for the human journey. In sharing, I hope to awaken each human individual to the other part of their self, a self that is perfect, created perfectly. I know that the wisdom for each individual resides within. At the same time, I realise that everything is divine and has a divine order, purpose, and time. May you come to know that all has been created in balance and harmony for each of us and our life journey experience.

It is the loving of everyone I work with and all who is another part of me that I wish to share what I know, what I have been given, my insights, and my interpretations of the law of attraction and beyond.

By knowing these better, perhaps more can have a joyous and happy life, knowing everything and everyone is being beautifully looked after. And knowing everything is in divine order.

There is so much joy for me when a client or student realises the abundant information and help Divine Source has provided. Information is provided for their self-realisation, as they reconnect in awareness to their divine nature. And they recognise the power within us all that is not only personal power but spiritual in nature.

As a teacher past and present, I know we all learn differently. We take in information and interpret it differently and thereby come to understand differently. Some know and understand the law of attraction just as it has been presented to them. Some may benefit from a different perspective. I give it here.

I share my understanding, insights, and knowledge of these universal laws and their effects on us all in the human condition. It is my perspective, through my eyes, mind, and experiences, that I offer here. Take them as you will, for you are free to do so.

Whenever I teach spirituality, whether in a workshop, class, or one-to-one, I begin with a Buddha quote, for I wish to convey my respect for each person's right of choice.

This is also an acknowledgement of where each person is at, where they are regarding their understanding of any information, their life experience, and the knowledge they already have on any subject matter from their personal perspective.

"Believe nothing,

No matter where you read it,

Or who said it,

No matter if I have said it,

Unless it agrees with your own reason

And your own common sense."

—Buddha

Dr. Elizabeth Conway

CONTENTS

INTRODUCTION

Have you heard of *The Secret* and the law of attraction? Do you understand what the Secret is? You may know or have heard of the law of attraction. Have you been able to implement it? Do you want to know the what and how of the law of attraction?

What if you could understand *and* implement both into your life and more? There are so many more universal laws beyond the law of attraction.

Have you ever wanted to know more about the universe and universal laws? Have you ever wanted to be able to work with universal laws, to create a successful life experience? Are you a serious student of spirituality? Are you interested in connecting with your spirituality? This book will not only teach you universal spiritual concepts, it will also empower you with knowledge from understanding, knowledge that is beyond what you currently know. This book is all about understanding better how you create your life, both positively and negatively. By understanding more fully, perhaps even more clearly, you will be able to negotiate your life within these universal laws to fulfil your needs, wants, and desires for yourself. When you gain a fuller understanding of universal laws, you will be able to create a happier and more joy-filled life experience, one you wish for yourself: the wonderful life you deserve.

In this book, you will learn about three universal laws that will help you better understand the workings of the law of attraction. These three laws each impact the law of attraction in their own unique way. One law partners with the law of attraction, creating the environment for attraction; another powers it; and the third effectively propels what you want to you.

Other universal laws are included in this book; they will help you understand the power you have to create the life of your choosing.

It is time to re-establish, revisit, and reconnect with some other universal laws and principles beyond the law of attraction. It's time to learn how each can affect and enhance this journey called life. Just as there are natural laws governing the order of your physical world, there are universal laws governing your higher or spiritual self beyond the physical experience.

The laws of the universe exist for your benefit. They govern the human realm, maintaining balance and harmony. The laws are there to support the human journey. They do not dictate the journey. You do. You can do that from your human nature or from your spiritual self: your higher self. This higher self is one with the divine source. The divine source is pure and unconditional love, loving you at all times, seeing you only and always as you were created in the beginning, perfectly.

Divine Source Love, loving each one of us unconditionally, sees no judgement and wants only the best for us. This is how you too can be nonjudgemental for yourself and for others. Love everyone unconditionally.

Many avoid taking responsibility for their actions when those actions are deemed inappropriate or destructive. They often believe this is equal to admitting to their inadequacies. They do so from a place of fear and self-loathing, never realising the damage they are doing to themselves, mentally and emotionally.

Taking responsibility for your actions puts you in a powerful mastery position. Everything is a learning experience. And if you choose to take responsibility and learn, you truly can be the master of your destiny and your life journey experience. Through your life experiences, you can choose to learn or ignore the rich lessons available to you in every encounter. In some encounters, the lesson is easy to understand. In others, the learning information and understanding takes time, sometimes many years. Each exposure will bring you pleasure or pain, understanding and tolerance or further fear and self-doubt. The latter then often leads to judgement, blame, finding fault, and making yourself (or others) wrong and bad. This is never a place of mastery, although working through these issues will lead to self-mastery.

What if you can find a way to stop blaming yourself or making yourself wrong? Is it possible to stop judging and start living your life in joy? Have you yet to discover a life of happiness due to peace of mind? What would it mean for you to come to know that everything is taken care of, including your life, beautifully? Is this even possible, let alone a probable reality?

What is the benefit of knowing universal laws? Not just being aware of them or having information on them, but truly knowing them, so as to benefit your life journey, benefit yourself. You are not meant to suffer, unless that is what you choose to experience. You are reading this book because you have already chosen that you want a better life experience. You are searching for ways to discover how to make the most of this life you have been given. Perhaps you wish to experience a life of peace, a life of joy, and a life of love, including self-love. You have come to a place where pain, suffering, and yes, even self-loathing, assaults your sensibilities, and you believe this is no way to live. You believe there must be a better way.

Divine Source Love has given you paradise, given you a wondrous playground, and set you free to experience this physical reality, this Eden. Why do you choose pain and suffering? Is it perhaps because you don't know, don't realise, or don't believe you have a choice? Some inflict pain onto others, with disastrous consequences, in an insane attempt to ease their own pain. Is this also law of attraction?

I do not believe that is the case. There are many other universal laws in play, and these may better explain why these anomalies occur and how these resultant consequences unfold. Not every interaction is due to attraction. You do attract many experiences into your life, yet there are also other factors at play in the rich story of your human journey. Karma is one of them. When an innocent is abused on any level, it is not necessarily due to the law of attraction. To presume everything is due to this law is simplifying the complex nature of the human experience. This, in part, is due to the lack of knowledge of the many laws at work within our universe.

This book teaches three key universal laws that will help you gain a fuller understanding of the law of attraction:

- the law of cause and effect: This partners with the law of attraction.

- the law of belief: This powers the law of attraction.

- the law of love: This propels the law of attraction to you.

Knowledge of these three laws enables you to work with the law of attraction more efficiently for a richer, rewarding, success-filled life.

Other laws take you beyond the law of attraction:

- natural and universal laws: for an overall or general understanding of laws and their operations

- the law of mind: where the beginnings for creation attraction appear

- the law of creation: the how in the process of creating

Although you have your spiritual side and nature, you may not be aware that there are universal laws that govern that side of your nature. You have on this planet all you need to heal you, sustain you, and bring you a life of ease and joy. Why then do you live mostly in fear or spend your time with feelings of lack, even when there is obvious wealth all around you? You have all that you need within you, yet you seem not to know how to access your own wisdom.

What is it that God meant when he gave Moses his commandments, making loving ourselves the most important commandment of all? This first commandment has often been interpreted as loving others and forgetting self-love. The key message of loving self first is overlooked, even lost over time. Have you ever considered why this commandment was deemed the greatest above all others?

"You shall love your neighbour as yourself. There is none other commandment greater than these." (Mark 12:31)

You were created in love by love.

And so it is.

CHAPTER 1

Natural and Universal Laws

This is one of man's oldest riddles. How can the
independence of human volition be harmonized with
the fact that we are integral parts of a universe which
is subject to the rigid order of nature's laws?

—Max Planck, *Where Is Science Going?*

Oxford Dictionary

Law a rule enacted or customary in a community as
commanding or forbidding certain actions.

Natural existing in or caused by nature.

Universal of, belonging to or done etc. by all; applicable to
all cases.

Law Definitions

For the purposes of this book, I differentiate between natural and universal laws:

> *Natural laws* are the laws of the physical world around us. These include our earth and all life living with us in our world.

> *Universal laws* are understood to be the laws governing and affecting the physical from a nonphysical place, be it mind or spirit. Each in itself affects the physical as well as the nonphysical world.

In the Beginning

There is an order, a harmony in the world we live in: a natural order and symmetry. Nature has its seasons, order of growth, blossoming, evolution, and transformation. In the animal kingdom, each species moves to the rhythm of its ancestors, each affecting the evolution of future generations of their species.

Humankind also has its own seasonal evolution in birth, maturation, and death. For a variety of reasons, we humans need to better understand the world we inhabit, to learn from our surroundings. Perhaps our need to learn stems from the human nature we possess. Primal to this nature is the need to survive. Our survival is an instinct ingrained into our DNA. Imagine how our earliest ancestors would have observed experiences and then taught each following generation that art of survival. Those who survived longer than others sought to find ways and means to extend their own survival, along with those who were dear to them—their families and tribes. Recognising the nature of life around them, the processes and order of things, they were better equipped to survive. Humankind's natural curiosity leads each generation to uncover the nature of what has yet to be discovered, yet to be understood: why and how the world around us works in the way it does.

Over time, that curiosity has extended to look inward, to better understand ourselves and others. Perhaps it began with wanting to know why others behaved in certain ways. In doing so, it was realised to know the self was equally important (and perhaps even more so). By understanding one other, as well as the world around us, we may better navigate this place we have found ourselves in: this life and our physical experiences.

To better understand the world around us and ourselves, we only need to turn to the laws of nature, recognising therein the natural structure, order, and cycle of life. In the physical world, there are many laws that govern the order of the various areas within the physical realm. So too in the spiritual world are many universal laws that govern and maintain order of that which is beyond the physical.

Many are unaware of the order within our natural world and how that has a bearing on our lives. Although science is taught in our schools, it is often deemed beyond understanding or not interesting enough. However, everyone knows at least to some degree, if only through observation and experience, the nature of the world around them. Interest often is only gained when there is a need to know.

Science and Laws

As stated before, natural laws are laws within nature that maintain order in our physical world.

Universal laws bring order to the world within us, our minds, our thoughts, affecting the world without and around us.

I do not wish to make a scientist of you as you read this information. Rather, I do this to give you a background of how humankind has explored the world to better understand it. And in so doing, show what previous generations have discovered helps us all to better navigate our surroundings. As we observe what is around us, we make up our minds as to what it is we are seeing. By making sense of what we see or hear, we make it mean something for ourselves. This is often called perception.

As scientists, these men and women of learning wished to understand themselves and the world in which they lived. Each in their own ways uncovered various phenomena that they further explored, uncovering various natural laws. Over time, they came to see that the world and the parts within it had a symmetry and were balanced and in harmony within the aspects of nature. They identified laws that governed that balance and harmony. Some laws seemed basic in nature; some were hidden from view until eventually discovered. Each law had a differing degree of impact on our lives. Their discoveries helped scientists and then the general population to understand and navigate the world we all live in.

Sir Isaac Newton's discovery of the law of gravity, Madame Marie Curie's discovery of polonium and radium, and Thomas Edison's work with the incandescent light bulb and the phonograph all affected our lives in powerfully positive ways. In their own way, they examined laws and principles within nature that governed these phenomena. Many of you studied various basic natural laws in school; the law of gravity is one such law. Other laws of physics that you may be familiar with include the laws of motion, reflection, relativity, thermodynamics, and quantum mechanics. There are further laws within each of the various sciences, including chemistry laws, geography laws, and biology laws.

The story of Isaac Newton and the apple landing on his head is universally known. Whether he was daydreaming or just relaxing his mind, he was immediately intrigued as to why the apple fell. He came to the conclusion—now obvious to us all—that something caused that fall. And that something came to be known as gravity, a notion he apparently had been contemplating prior to the fall of the apple.

Why is it we don't fly like birds or float off the ground? Why is it that things fall to the ground? Other scientists must have been curious and contemplated similar notions as Newton did, yet he went further. He wanted to *know* and know *more*. He believed there must be a force that pulls objects, including us, downward, and the law of gravity was uncovered.

Although we have the law of gravity, humans have successfully flown, seemingly defying that law. Yet we didn't defy gravity. Rather someone uncovered another natural law to allow flight to be a reality for humans. Seeking to fly like a bird, individuals looked to the birds to understand how they achieved flight. Michelangelo often drew man with wings and winglike structures in an attempt to discover the secret to human flight. It was other natural laws that led to human flight. Gravity is not overcome to gain flight; rather, it is used for landing. So there is one law to fly and another to ensure we remain grounded.

Nature and the Universe

The law of gravity is a natural law, a scientific law of our natural world, governing our earth's atmosphere. The law of attraction is universal inasmuch as it governs our personal universe, universally. Was there gravity before Newton's discovery? Did it exist prior to his discovery? I'm sure some will argue the point philosophically, but there is no doubt people walked on the ground due to gravity's pull. It existed, whether or not it had been named. The world around us already had order and purpose, cycles, seasons, and reasons. It was up to humankind to make sense of it to successfully and happily survive in the world.

Natural laws exist to maintain order in the physical and natural worlds. Universal laws explain the workings of the nonphysical world, primarily the world of the mind.

Gravity was available to humans long before Newton discovered it, for it was always part of our atmosphere. So, too, the law of attraction was and is part of our universe. Who discovered the law of attraction is not known. However, the law was known to the mystics of old through their abilities to connect with the universe and its life force energy.

The law of attraction, like the law of gravity, works whether you are aware of it or not. Until Newton discovered the law of gravity, did it exist? Of course! Apples fell out of trees, yet no one took particular notice until Newton came along. The law of attraction is the same. It has been working in your life and doesn't need your knowledge of it to exist. The law is of the universe, not of you. Knowing about it just makes it easier for you to work with the universe for your benefit. The universe and its laws were set up to serve you throughout your life experience.

Although gravity exists, humankind is seemingly able to defy gravity and fly. Why? Because someone understood other scientific laws that made it possible to fly. The law of aerodynamics is one example. So, too, can we, with the knowledge and understanding of other laws of the universe, align ourselves with the law of attraction for our benefit. Knowing how to align ourselves with the universe and its laws is the first step to being able to work with these laws. We cannot manipulate universal laws, just as we cannot manipulate any natural laws. Although it may seem so, in some instances, it is always the use of another law that may make it seem like a law is being overridden. What alignment means and how it is achieved is valuable information in understanding how to work with universal laws for our betterment. Sometimes it is another law that will achieve a preferred outcome rather than the law of attraction.

Laws in General

We are all familiar with the laws that govern our society, our community, and our country. If you belong to a sports team, a religious group, or any other organisation, they all have their set of rules and laws you are expected to abide by. Even family membership and friendship connections have their own conditions and requirements. Many laws are written down. Others are unspoken yet no less considered and expected to be adhered to by those in the group. They are the understood parameters and boundaries that govern the members of the group, maintaining order and compliance of those involved, even if only in presumption. This is to maintain harmony and balance for all in the group. In developing a law, the overriding assumption is that it provides order for its members and prevents disturbance and disharmony. As there is law and order in our natural physical world, it seems to make sense to have law and order in our social world. Without realising, humankind has set in place their own individual laws, often unaware that the universe has already in place universal laws that also govern our personal and social order, balance, and harmony. Several of these are discussed in the following chapters.

These laws have been part of our history since the earliest of times. The mystics of old, the metaphysicians dating back to Aristotle and Socrates, all knew of the universal laws that govern our lives; they wrote about them often. Out of their work of observation and discovery were born the sciences of today. The various fields of study were delineated into the specific areas of study and specialisation (physics, chemistry, biology, mathematics, geology, etc.). They chose to study these to know the how, what, and why of their particular field of interest. And over time, each area of the sciences uncovered natural laws that helped maintain order within our world.

The Human Condition

Humankind has always had a deep need to know itself and the world. How do we best fit into that world, who we are in this world, and finally, how do we want to live in it? Many are curious of the world around them, wanting to discover the seen and unseen world. They also want to uncover why they themselves as well as others behave a certain way. Wanting to know more, they search for the meaning and workings of the mind, discovering therein its natural (often referred to as universal) laws.

We observe, perceive, and theorise on our world, others, and ourselves all the time. Perhaps the level of curiosity, a wanting to know, is within us all. You may not have known that you too are a student of science. Yet it is not only our curiosity that has moved us forward in life. It is also our instinct for survival. We need to know the world, all it contains, and how it gives us the vital information we need for our survival. Knowing what land to live on, which will ensure not only our comfort but our survival, is crucial. We need to know what food to eat and what is not poisonous. Knowing what people to befriend and trust is in our DNA from the days of our ancestors.

Knowing ourselves better is another level of universal information that ensures not only our survival but one in which we flourish. Our ancestors fought to survive, and their legacy lives on in us all. Now the lay of the land, the food we digest, and the people we need to protect ourselves from is not the world without but the world within. Fear, ego, false belief systems, and self-deprecation are our true enemies of mass destruction. The lay of the land is our mind. The food we digest is for our survival. The food of mind is our thoughts. What do we feed our minds with? Are the thoughts of love or fear? The person we look at with fear is our own ego. The person we are willing to love is our true self. All thoughts of fear are due to a level of ignorance and unawareness. With good information, we gain understanding. With understanding comes knowledge. Self-knowledge brings with it self-mastery. Spiritual self-knowledge awakens within us the consciousness that we have nothing to fear, not even death.

Knowledge, it is said, is power. And many people believe they have knowledge when what they truly have is information. Information, when acted upon, brings about better understanding of that information. When there is actioning of any information to understand it, in that understanding, knowledge is born.

As human beings, we can work with natural or universal laws, or we may seem to work against them. We can do so in awareness or in unawareness, unconsciously reacting to the world around us. This then impacts our world within ourselves, creating for us a view of the world without. Or we can move beyond the human, transcending it by connecting with the divine source mind. This is where your genius resides. This is where the wisdom for your self is housed, ever waiting for the time, the day, the hour you become whole, once more in awareness of your connection with the Divine Source Mind.

I am forever grateful to the men and women of learning, the curiosity seekers, the thinkers, the explorers, the adventurers, and yes, even the rebels. They each in their own way have paved the way for us to better understand and enjoy the world we have today.

Channelled Insight

When the two worlds of illusion and reality collide,

then you will know the value of these laws in place for you,

each in their own unique way protecting and providing what is needed for your knowing.

Divine Source Love built a world, a universe, a playground,

safe for your playing,

safe for your learning,

safe for your eternal returning,

ever evolving, infinitely being

that which is the beginning,

for the purposes of no ending.

In understanding this, comes the understanding of being.

Affirmations

Affirmation statements work best when

- you believe in the statement, at least on some level,

- they are set in the now, and

- they are said or written, adding power to the vibrational energy of the affirmation.

Affirmations Statements

- In all things I am in balance and harmony with the world and this universe.

- I love, appreciate, and accept all that is in the natural world that surrounds me.

- I am at one with the earth, the sea, the sky, and the animals of this planet.

- I lovingly enjoy all that this earth provides abundantly to and for me.

- I share in the riches of this planet.

- I am given much in abundantly blessed experiences in this human journey.

- I enjoy all that is available to me from my world.

Follow-Up Tasks

- Note your thoughts and feelings regarding the natural world around you.

- Are you in fear of any part of the natural world? Look to the reasons for your fears.

- Discover if you are governed mostly by your fears or by the laws of love.

- Discover the laws that govern your everyday behaviour and interaction with others.

- Note what information you are processing in your mind, with the knowledge that it will impact how you see the world around you. Is the information positive or negative?

CHAPTER 2

The Law of Attraction

Like Thought Attracts Like Thought

"What you love, you empower.

And what you fear, you empower.

And what you empower, you attract."

—Unknown

Oxford Dictionary

Attraction 1 a. attracting or being attracted. b. attractive quality (*can't see the attraction in it*), c. person or thing that attracts. **2** *Physics* tendency of bodies to attract each other.

Law Definition

Your thoughts, either positive or negative, will attract (draw to you) people, events, and experiences that have the same like thought.

Spiritually speaking, you manifest your thoughts into your reality. You are the creator of your life and the experiences therein (see chapter 7).

The Law of Attraction

The law of attraction has become widely known today due to the film *The Secret* and the works of Esther and Jerry Hicks through Esther's channel, Abraham. They opened up the minds of many to this most powerful of universal laws.

Before Esther and Jerry Hicks, many people knew and wrote about this universal law. Yet the law of attraction is not the only universal law that exists, although it is a most powerful one. While many have heard of the law of attraction, few truly understand how it works. Even fewer know how they can work within this law to make their life experience one that is richer, more rewarding, and more fulfilling.

The universal law of attraction simply described is also the law that explains your life and why it is unfolding as it has. You have attracted the people and experiences of your life to you. Can it be that simple? And knowing this, do you look at your life and question why negative experiences have been attracted into your life? Do you admonish yourself or call yourself bad for having this knowledge? If so, let me encourage you to have no judgement and place no blame upon your life, your self, or your experiences.

And at the same time, I also encourage you to make no judgement or place no blame on another. This is not the energy alignment that will empower you to attract good into your life. Everything is as it is meant to be for learning and growth, not for blame and certainly not as a punishment. The universe does not deal in blame, judgement, or punishment. We as humans do a very good job on all these levels for ourselves. You have become expert enough in this area. You are then left with fear and ego as your companions. The time has come for us all to be in alignment with the universe and attract the love, balance, and harmony the universe provides.

Just as gravity is not the only law of nature, so too you are not just a magnet attracting everything or anything to yourself. If gravity were the only law of nature, humankind would have never found a way to fly. So too, if the law of attraction were the only universal law, you would never have been able to experience a life filled with miraculous experiences.

Knowing how to align yourself with the universe and its laws is the first step to being able to work with these laws. What alignment means and how it is achieved is valuable information, information for you to understand how it is possible to work with universal laws for your betterment.

Having more information, more knowledge, gives you a better insight for understanding. These are the building blocks for your self-development. Perspectives and experiences from others all add to the enrichment of your life. I am not advocating accepting another's perspective or experience as your own. Rather, consider it as another insight worthy of analysis and evaluation for its significance to you and your life experience. Consider the value of having the information for understanding other laws. Universal laws enable you to gain a clearer understanding of better reception for attraction and how to align with what you want.

As you come to learn more about other universal laws, I trust you will come to better understand the law of attraction. By having a working understanding of this universal knowledge, you will be able to enhance and enrich your life experience. Most importantly, it will give you skills and tools, empowering you to be in charge of your life, in control of your life rather than a bystander, in command of your life rather than waiting and responding to life's circumstances. Take back control as the driver and navigator of your life experiences rather than being just the passenger.

To be able to align with the universe, you must first understand how to connect with it. You do this by connecting your energy with the universe's. This connection is achieved through aligning your vibrational energy with that of the universe. To be able do this, it is important to have an understanding of energy and the thing called vibration.

Energy and Vibration

> "Energy cannot be created or destroyed; it can only be changed from one form to another."

> —Albert Einstein

What is energy but a power source in action? Everything is energy and energy vibration. Everything is vibration at a particular rate or speed, often call frequency.

You are energy. That energy has power. That power is yours, is you.

Think of energy as a wave vibration. Electricity is a form of energy current that humans are able to harness. That energy current gives you the electric light and electricity to power your modern-day lifestyle. Electricity is the source you harness for many of your power needs.

Consider all the devices you have the use of due to the discovery of electricity and its power (light, computer, TV, radio).

Each device taps into the electricity source through a particular frequency or energy vibration. When you turn on your radio or TV, you tune into a particular channel. How is it possible to even have the various channels that you select? It is because each has its own frequency wave vibration that it uses to allow you to connect with any particular device or channel.

There are many forms of energy other than electricity. The sun, water, wind, coal, oil, natural gas, and nuclear energy are all energy sources. Furthermore, there are different frequencies that exist in the air (or ether). Sound, light, radio, and even the brain has its own frequency, its own oscillating current.

The law of gravity cannot be influenced to be or do other than what it was created for. So too the law of attraction cannot be controlled. Once you are in awareness of the law of attraction, all you need to remember is to be in vibrational alignment (be the frequency) with your desires or wants. Then that which is like your desire will come to you.

Just as the radio or TV is not the source of its electricity, just the receiver, you receive your power from the divine source. You are just the receiver and perceiver of your manifestations. The main source of energy for all that you wish to create is sourced from what is often called the universal life force. I like to call it Divine Source. You do need to be connected to the right frequency and be switched on to be able to harness the power of this main source. You are always connected to the main power grid. However, you need to be connected to the right frequency and be switched on to be able to harness the energy from the main power source, just as any receiver in nature does.

The Divine Source/Universal Intelligence (universal mind) is the main power source of the all and beyond. When you harness that power, you have the energy to use, create, and manifest all your needs, wants and desires.

Once you are in awareness of the law of attraction, all you need to do is be in vibrational alignment with what you desire (i.e., the frequency) for that which is like your desire to come to you. Just as the radio or TV has various stations, so too does your subconscious mind. It is the sender and the receiver. As the receiver, what channel are you tuned into? As the sender, what message are you sending out into the world?

Magnetic Energy and Magnetic Field

A magnetic field is the area around an object that creates a magnetic attraction or magnetised effect on another magnet or magnetic field. What makes this happen is the energy or electric current within each object. In a scientific physical explanation of what happens with magnets and magnetic fields, you have electric currents and moving electrical particles creating magnetic energy and energy fields. These are pulling the magnetic energy of currents and fields in line with your own. This is often referred to as your vibration. You would have already experienced these energy fields. How often do you feel good around one person yet uncomfortable in the presence of someone else? You are picking up on, sometimes even feeling, their energy field.

Personal Energy and Energy Vibration

You as energy are sending out your energy vibrations, or vibes, at all times. As you send your vibes out, similar vibrations are drawn to you, like a magnet. These like vibrations connect with yours, amplifying your energy vibration, at any and all points in time. In other words, if you are feeling happy or sad, that vibration is amplified by a similar feeling in the ether of the planet.

Sometimes, you may not even be feeling particularly happy or sad, yet your mood seems to change. You have responded to the energy vibrations of others. This is most noticeable when you first wake up and immediately feel either happy or sad, with no noticeable outside influence other than this feeling comes over you. You are responding to a like energy that is out there in kind.

Similarly, whether you are sad or happy, this vibration goes out into the atmosphere, into the universe, where others can pick it up. This also makes it possible for another like vibration to tap into your vibration, amplifying it and returning it to you in manifested reality. This all often happens while you are sleeping. In other words, it occurs while you were not paying attention to yourself or your thoughts. It is happening within your subconscious mind. However, you can consciously choose to be the positive vibration energy that creates a positive effect in your life. You do this by being in conscious awareness, rather than unconscious unawareness.

Your Personal Power

You now understand energy to be a power source: the source that generates power. But what about the power source that is you? You are energy, and that energy has power, although you are not the main source of your power. You derive your power from universal intelligence. Just as food fuels the energy your body needs, the universal life force energy is the main energy fuel source of your mind's power. You can harness that power to use in any way you choose. It can be for help and guidance, or to manifest your wants, needs, and desires. By tapping into (connecting with) the universal mind/intelligence, you are able to create the reality of your dreams, working for your highest good and the highest good of others.

How you choose to use that source fuel is your choice, as you have been given free will to choose.

You are able to harness that power to

- manifest your desires or demons,

- enable connection with universal mind/intelligence for your higher intelligence and insight or to further fuel your ego,

- stay in the mindset of your true self or of being "only human,"

- create your life, working for your highest good and the highest good of others, or continue to recreate your past,

- make you believe you are destructible and have no power or choice in your life,

- have the power to believe in untruths, where others have the control over you, and

- know the truth and positive power of you.

Your Magnetic Energy Field

Like a magnet, you attract to yourself what you are magnified for. The vibrational energy you are emanating creates a force field that pulls or repels people or events reflecting your like thoughts. Just as an energy battery has two or more electromagnetic cells, our body's energy field contains positive and negative energy vibrational cells.

The power of the mind causes the body to vibrate at any particular level. What is the vibration your energy field is emanating from your body? What are your thoughts, words, and actions? What do you think about regarding money, family, health, work, love, and yourself? Knowing your thoughts, your true thoughts, around these and other issues will clarify for you, in part, what and why you have the life you are experiencing.

How do you measure the intensity of your field attraction? Do you know how to discover what you are attracting in your life and why? There is one simple technique you can use to uncover your vibrational pull. Ask yourself if you are in fear or in love regarding any issue at hand. What are your feelings regarding an issue, situation, or person? What is your subconscious or unconscious mindset around the issue, situation, or person? You may feel one way consciously. However, is your subconscious mind in agreement with the conscious mind? And how do you discover what your subconscious mind thinks? The best way is to check your belief systems (see chapter 3). Are you feeling fearful, anxious, angry, or upset? Or are you feeling loving and at peace toward the issue, event, or person? You will then immediately know what vibration you are emanating and what you are attracting (or are likely to attract) to yourself.

"If you've got somebody's aspects in your experience that you don't like, there's only one reason they're there, you keep evoking them with your attention to them. Without knowing about the Law of Attraction, you have through your old habits of observation achieved vibrational harmony with the parts of them that you do not like, and you keep summoning those parts from them by your constant vibrational offering to them."—Abraham

The Power to Attract or Repel

What are your feelings around money? Are they positive or negative? Check if you believe you have enough. You may know its value to you intellectually and desire more in your life. You may even know without a doubt that you deserve to be wealthy, yet you have not been able to attract wealth into your life. Or maybe you have, but somehow it seemed to slip through your fingers. You may have learnt money is evil or it will corrupt or it is out of your reach or there is not enough of it to go around. Or you may believe that having too much money is somehow bad or wrong. These thoughts will certainly demagnetise the energy you need to attract wealth.

It is important you check the feelings, belief systems, ideas, perceptions, and opinions you have around money (or any other desire you wish to attract into your life). In this awareness, you will glean the insight needed into the thoughts that create your energy vibration for attraction. You will attract lack or abundance of the very thing you desire.

If you recognise that your thoughts are positive, check the intensity of your vibration. You can do this by assessing your feelings around the issue. Are your feelings cool, mildly warm, or passionately intense? This then gives you the indication of your frequency for attraction. In doing so, make sure you are honest with yourself. The subconscious mind is powerful and often works to delude you into believing something other than your true, underlying thought system.

Of course, you can replace the word "money" with anything you wish to attract into your life (weight loss, finding your life partner, getting the job of your dreams, or attaining the life of your dreams); check your vibrational alignment in the same way. In checking your thoughts for frequency alignment, remember to check the underlying subconscious thoughts, emotions, feelings, and belief systems. Be honest with yourself. You will thank yourself for that honesty, as you will know the true vibrational alignment you are in. With that accurate information, you can clear any negative fields within you. Then you are ready to recharge your energies and thereby realign your magnetic field for that which you choose to attract.

As I have stated before all too often, the law of attraction is discussed as if it were the only universal law in existence. It may be the only one you know extensively, as other universal laws are rarely talked about. You can only work with what you have.

It is time for uncovering, discovering, and learning (or relearning), beyond this one universal law. Now you know there are many laws governing the order, balance, and harmony to the physical realm through the nonphysical realm. As knowledge of the natural physical laws helped us all to better navigate our physical world, it was only a part of the equation.

In our human world, only a few people are scientists, wishing to have detailed and specialised scientific knowledge. So too in the world of metaphysics: Only a few truly want to know themselves fully through the laws that govern the universe.

You do not need to be a scientist to know the detailed workings of electricity, TV, or the Internet. For most of us, it is enough to know the basics so that we can make the best use of these devices for a better life. These devices can make your life better, easier, and more fun.

You do not need to be a mystic or metaphysician to work with the universe for a better life experience. However, having some basic knowledge of how the devices of the mind work will make for a better, easier, and more enjoyable life.

Who would not want their life to be richer, more joyful, and filled with wonderful experiences? Few would argue with that, particularly seeing the scientific discoveries over the last hundred years and the positive impact these discoveries have had on our lives. So too the knowledge of the universal laws of the unseen world of the mind will empower you and your life for the better.

At the same time, know that Divine Source is looking after everyone, particularly you. The universe and its laws have been set up for your use, although you can also confidently rely on your angels, guides, and divine source love to be ever present in supporting your life journey and experiences.

"The great error of the present day is the idea that man has to originate the intelligence whereby the Infinite can proceed to bring about a specific purpose or result. Nothing of this kind is necessary; the Universal Mind can be depended upon to find the ways and means for bringing about any necessary manifestation. We must, however create the ideal, and this ideal should be perfect."—Charles F. Haanel

You and the Law

There are many who truly understand what is meant by the law of attraction; they do not confuse occurrences of this law. It is time for awareness, for light to be shed on other universal laws that govern your world within. Knowing how to align yourself with the universe and its laws is the first step to being able to work with these laws.

To get what you want, you must have the best connection for the best reception of your desire. This is so you can better know which frequency within your self to tune into, to not only be the receiver but to clearly send out your message: your hopes and desires. You now know that to get what you want, you must have the best connection for the best reception for your wants and desires. Remember: You also will be drawn to the magnetic field or magnetism of others. That which you wish or have a strong desire for is what will draw you to them. Just as you can attract others, so too can others attract you to them.

The law of attraction is an important and powerful law to be aware of. Knowing this law enables you to realise how much control you have in your life. At the same time, you come to see where you are not in control. Your life is not controlled by others or even the universe, although it may seem like that at times. In fact, you are the most powerful influence in your own life (see chapter 7). Knowing the law of attraction should give you hope, for you can take back control. You are the one attracting people, events, situations, and occurrences to yourself. Once you know how this is happening, you can learn to work with the law for your betterment.

You cannot manipulate any law, natural or universal. Nevertheless, you can work with any law to gain what you wish for your life. If you're aware of these laws, you will then know which to use in any particular circumstance you wish to experience. It is that simple. Knowing more about the three key laws that influence the law of attraction will better help you work with the universe for your happiness. Each of these laws have an effect in understanding the law better and in helping you work to transcend the law, where or when necessary. You will benefit from the knowledge of three specific laws that influence in the law of attraction. The law of cause and effect partners with the law of attraction; this is the cause of that which is attracted to you by your very vibration. The law of belief gives power to the law of attraction, for what you believe is what you truly attract. And the law of love propels that which you desire to you.

Knowing the existence of universal laws is the first step towards understanding them and being able to work with them. Universal laws are designed and put into place for your benefit. Being aligned and in harmony with universal laws enriches your life experience, bringing with it self-growth, self-evolution, along with self-mastery.

Channelled Insight

So much has been said already on this subject that I have little to add, except the misinterpretation of this understanding we have shared with the writings here.

God has not created anything to make you feel wrong and bad. These are just structures in place so you don't lose your way.

Everything is not as it seems, and nothing is as simple as you wish to make it, yet it is simple to the world of spirit. You have complicated the simple but want to understand it simply. Simple is best, yet you have not understood the best.

Affirmation Statements

- I acknowledge the divine source power within.

- I work for my highest good.

- I attract all that I need for all that I want.

- I am one with my desires.

- I attract all that is of benefit for my life journey.

- I am at one with and in awareness of my higher self.

- I am aligned with my desired intent.

Follow-Up Tasks

- Know clearly, even write down, what you wish to attract into your life.

- For each item, know clearly why you wish to attract it into your life.

- Discover your subconscious feelings regarding that which you wish to attract into your life.

- Decide if your subconscious is in alignment or not with that which you desire to attract.

- Work to bring yourself into alignment with your heart's desires, be it through positive affirmations, overcoming fears and ego, or working with your mind to reprogram your subconscious sabotage programming.

CHAPTER 3

The Law of Belief

The Law that Partners with the Law of Attraction

Believing Is Seeing

"Whatever the mind can conceive and believe it can achieve."

—Napoleon Hill, *Think and Grow Rich*

Oxford Dictionary

Belief firm opinion; acceptance (*that is my belief*)

Law Definition

What you believe becomes your manifested reality.

What Do You Believe?

Is the sky blue, grey, red, yellow, or green? Do you sit on a table or a chair? Is the person who raised you your parent? Are all who eat vegetables vegetarians?

Whatever you answered, have you ever considered why it is that you answer the way you do?

Let's look at the question regarding the colour of the sky. This question is asked, knowing that colours are due to a reality, a reality that at one point in time the concept of colour was considered and names for each spectrum of light were then agreed upon. Even so, there are some who see colour differently (or so it seems), for they are what is called colour blind. Those who are not believe they see colour the same as another. Even then, there are times when you may see a shade of colour differently. Why is this, if we see things like colour the same? What if we don't all see the same? However, for better interactions with each other, agreement in language terms is essential. Understanding the physical world around us (a tree is a tree is a tree) makes connecting with each other easier. Problems or conflict often arise when there is no agreement with what is being viewed by separate parties or we *believe* differently.

Beliefs

You hold many beliefs in and around various aspects of your life: of people, of situations, and in particular of yourself. You may consciously be aware of some of these beliefs; however, many are set deep within your subconscious mind. You often respond automatically to most of your life events and situations. This you do depending on your beliefs about what you are experiencing, in any particular moment in time.

A belief is only an opinion, yet many people seem to think a belief is also a truth, a truth that most have not tested the validity of. Most people do not pay attention to their thoughts, let alone whether what they believe in is based on fact. Deep within your subconscious mind are belief systems that you no longer question the validity of.

You believe that what you *see* is reality, the real world. However, you are seeing your world through your particular personal perception:

your judgements, your prejudices, your bias, your values, your impressions, your interpretations, and your fears.

"There is no reality only perception."—Dr. Phil McGraw

In his book *Understand Psychology,* Nicky Hayes states, "Perception is all about interpreting the information that the mind receives from the outside world, and working out what it means." You perceive through each of your senses: sight, sound, smell, taste, and touch, making it mean something particular.

You and Belief

You cannot and will not attract that which you desire into your life while you have an opposing thought belief. You may think you want wealth (or any other desire) yet you may believe having wealth is not possible for you on some level. Often this thought belief is deep within your subconscious mind. However when you have a belief system in opposition to your true desires, you negate that which your heart truly wants.

You repeatedly take on a belief or create a belief system without ever testing the validity of that belief. This begins from the time you are born; these early childhood years are when you develop many beliefs that become part of your navigational system. Some beliefs are truths indeed; however, many have been interpreted incorrectly. Over time, few people look to their beliefs or those of others. Many beliefs are not only false but disempowers the believer.

Some of these beliefs are learnt in early childhood:

- I am not loveable.

- I am not good enough.

- I am not good at sport, singing, art, and so on.

- I am not worthy to be loved, liked, given wealth. Etc.

Once a belief is in place, people with any negative beliefs will live into that belief, making it true for themselves, rather than it being true. There are many factors other than early childhood learning. There is your ongoing learning and programming of belief over your lifetime. Your experiences and how you perceive and interpret them are often transformed into new beliefs.

As an alternative therapist and metaphysical professional, I found that whatever problem, disease, or trauma a client came to me with inevitably exposed some false belief system or a lack of self-belief. It became evident over time working with each client where these false and self-defeating beliefs originated. Few of these beliefs were ever tested for validity, but they had become truths for my clients. Fear and ego were both used as protection mechanisms against a hostile world they had come to believe to be real.

Your beliefs either enhance or lower your self-esteem. There are many causes of action (see chapter 7) open to you to build self-belief, leading you to a healthier and happier self-actualised state.

Knowing and recognising the value of your true self, particularly from a metaphysical or spiritual perspective, gives you a more powerful and profound insight into who you truly are. This discovery is an effective base in building a strong self-belief structure.

Self-awareness, through self-discovery, will help you to recognise your self-concept. The concept you have of yourself will reveal the level of self-belief you have. This is not the same as having ego or being egotistic. The building of self-esteem through self-awareness brings with it the understanding of what you are attracting or repealing from your life experiences and why. There are many aspect of your self that impact your belief in yourself. Self-concept relies on the view you have of yourself. Is the view clear or cloudy: clouded by others' views and opinions, judgement, blame, shame, and punishment? Or do you truly love yourself, regardless of any mistakes, errors, or failed attempts at some life experience? All these impact your judgement of your worth. Yet how can you love the self you deem less than? Have you ever questioned your self-beliefs? If so, have you lived into those beliefs, making them real to somehow prove your theory of being unworthy? Do you blame others for their part in your low self-esteem? What if you knew in truth you were much greater than you believe possible? Would you then be able to live into your greatness? Whatever your current reality, based on some belief past or present, you can change that belief. Just remember: beliefs not truths.

Beliefs and Your Power

It is important to evaluate the truth of a belief in this way:

- Identify if this belief/opinion holds true, in this now moment.

- Determine if the belief empowers or disempowers you.

In this context, disempowerment means a disconnection you have from your own personal power. You will always know the answer to these questions. Ask yourself, "Am I better for having this belief or not? Is this belief true or just an illusion I have come to falsely believe in?" You will know the answers to these questions from how you feel when you ask them. You will feel fearful or not, full of energy or depleted in the thought of the belief. These are genuine indicators as to whether the belief is empowering or disempowering.

It is often said of people who are not feeling empowered that they are giving their power away.

I have never been able to fully relate to this concept. I do understand why it is being said. This is generally how people feel when they believe they are powerless. Power is the ability to do or act, to influence and to have energy. When you are overwhelmed by another and do not act or react, you may feel you are not being in your power. This often is because of something you believe about yourself, the other person, or the situation you find yourself in. Know that you are made of energy, and energy cannot be destroyed. If you believe you are giving away something that is intrinsically yours, you are believing in an illusion and not reality. Science has discovered the truth about energy: Energy cannot be destroyed. Therefore, it cannot be given away, either. You have our own energy vibration. You have your own power, which is yours; it cannot be destroyed or given away. Like a finger or arm, it is part of you; it is you. You feel powerless because you are disconnected from that which you have, disconnected from the only place you can be disconnected, your mind, within your thoughts. In awareness, you are once more made aware and can easily reconnect with your power within.

When you feel powerless, it is usually because

- you are not aware of your own power,

- you are not using your power,

- you don't know how best to use it, or

- all of the above.

Check your belief systems. Test them. Then decide which to keep because they empower you and you are empowered or energised by them, for your good and the good of the all.

The beliefs you discover are disempowering you and worthy of letting go are those that

- are not in your best interest,

- are found not to be true,

- once were true (or may have been true) but no longer are, or

- no longer "serve" you (they have no value to and for you).

When you begin examining your belief systems, you may also discover where they originated. You will come to realise that some were imposed from your cultural background, from society, or from the many influencers in your life. The time has come for you to determine which beliefs are true for you, now. Consider the life you wish to have, the life you wish to attract, the life you choose to manifest into reality. It must be a life you believe will be yours or is possible to be yours. It is important to let go of your false beliefs and replace them with beliefs that are true and worthy of the truth of you. Ultimately, you need to believe in you.

Belief and Affirmations

As you have come to understand, consciously or unconsciously, you have many belief systems. They either enhance your life or disable you in some way. Discovering your belief systems and deciding if they are valid will help you let go of that which no longer serves you.

The power of an affirmation to work, or not, is dependant on a universal law: the law of belief. An affirmation, if said in a state of belief, allows the law of attraction to go into action to provide more of that which the believer believes. Saying something without believing it is like trying to trick yourself and the universe into believing it. It can't be done, and the truth is always revealed. Your perceived truth in the form of your belief systems creates your illusionary reality. Changing your beliefs will change your reality.

Saying affirmations is an excellent way to change an ingrained belief system. However, when changing one belief for another, you have to convince your subconscious mind to believe in this new belief. And it is not easily fooled. It is there for your protection and does its job very well.

You may wish to have more money in your life and repeat an affirmation to make this a reality. You may say the following affirmation: "I have financial abundance in my life."

If your mindset really is "I don't have enough money. I want more," while you're thinking this, it is also what energy vibration you are emanating and what you are attracting. This is called a lack mentality. Words are only as powerful as the truth within the thought of the words. You may not be aware of this, but your subconscious thought is more powerful than your affirmation. And these thoughts are vibrating more powerfully than the words within an affirmation you do not yet believe in.

If your mindset is "I have all that I need, including money, in this moment in time," then the affirmation of financial abundance vibration is heard. It is in alignment with your unconscious mind, as well as the conscious. The universe then sets out to deliver situations, events, and people to make that your new reality.

Know that in reality, you do have enough and always will. This is particularly true for most of the people living in the Western world.

The universe, Divine Source Love, is looking after us always and in all ways and always.

Some affirmations are worded safely for the ego. The human fear ego mind is within our subconscious and unconscious mind. It is the mind that will not accept an affirmation it does not believe in. Presenting it with a new thought that appeases its sensibility is the key to changing your mindset with positive affirmations.

Here are some examples:

- In each moment of time, I acknowledge I am given all that I need.

- I happily receive all that I need, now and always.

- I learning now receive all that I need and more.

- I am grateful for all that I am given.

Gratitude is a powerful receiver.

Your Beliefs and Spiritual Awareness

What is it that you believe? You may not know this, but your belief system is what powers you. Finding out what you believe in and what you believe to be true motivates (powers) your actions and how you view your life and your life experiences. How you view your reality, how you perceive the world around you, is primarily based on what you believe regarding what you see. You would have often heard "Seeing is believing"; however, what is more likely to be the case is "Believing is seeing."

In spiritual terms, you may have heard that this life, the one you are living now, is an illusion, although to you it looks, tastes, smells, sounds, and feels very real to you (just like in a dream). You may have even heard this life experience referred to as a dream state, that you are only dreaming this life and that it is possible to awaken from this dream into reality. Just think about the times when you remember your dream. Upon waking up, you realised it was a dream. Yet while you were dreaming, it felt real. And although you were dreaming, in the remembering, you are the viewer of the events unfolding. What if you are aware that you are only dreaming? Could you change your dream and create a scenario of your choosing? Some say they have done just that while they were dreaming.

Carl Jung, the renowned psychologist, had a particular perspective on dreams and dreaming. He believed that the dream had a message for the dreamer and that the unconscious or subconscious brain was trying to tell the conscious brain something. And he felt that that message was always of benefit, in one form or another, for the dreamer. It may clarify a concern, give input for a problem's solution, or offer insight for the dreamer. He believed the best person to identify the dream's meaning was always the dreamer, but a skilled dream therapist could help dreamers discover their own answers. Next time you remember a dream, seek to discover the unconscious revelation for yourself of the dream's message.

Again consider if this life is just a dream and you, the dreamer dreaming it? Do you just play a part as an observer, just following the dream as it is played out before you? Or do you step into the dream and make it go the way you want it to be? As it unfolds, do you accept the role you have, or are you willing to change an outcome by changing the sequence of events? At different times, are you the observer and also the creative dream maker? Are you able to decide, as in a dream, the way your life is to unfold and decide on the dream you choose for your life?

Isn't it interesting how you are encouraged to dream big, to pursue your dreams, your dream partner, or your dream job? Do you believe your dreams can come true? Have yours come true? Did you believe they could? And what of those who follow their dreams, who are referred to as dreamers, as if they aren't living in reality? And what is reality, in truth, but only your perception of it?

Self-Belief

In today's world, where stress, anxiety, depression, and suicide are increasing, it is my contention that self-belief is paramount. Why is there such a high rate of suicide? Why do people in the affluent Western world experience extreme levels of stress and anxiety? Perhaps we are hearing more about these conditions through modern media networks. It may be because these conditions were not recognised or diagnosed in the past. Why do they exist in a world with so many resources and such advanced technology? Where did these conditions originate? What is the root cause of distress and disease? How can we avoid distress, anxiety, and depression? Is it even possible to live a stress-free life of joy and happiness? Are there certain triggers that set off (or even create) stress and anxiety? Are particular people predisposed to distress and disease, or is everyone subject to them? Is it possible to eliminate these states of angst? What is the best course of action to effect a more positive outcome in people's lives? Is there a *How to Live Distress and Disease Free* manual? Where do you search for answers? More importantly, how is it that among a community of the faithful, who believe in a higher power, God, many are still gripped with fears, doubts, and insecurities? Whatever the reasons, the facts remain that there is more distress than ever before, with higher levels of stress and new diseases being discovered.

The answers to these questions are vital for me in my work as an educator and metaphysical practitioner. Discovering the answers is critical to a healthy and satisfactory outcome for my clients. Although there may be many variables along with different solutions, the source of all begins in the mind of the believer. It is there where the answers will be found.

Having a belief (or believing in something) is a general concept regarding people, situations, and the self. Self-belief is having a positive self-concept, holding high self-esteem, and believing in your own worth. People usually have various beliefs about their self, both positive and negative, that impact their level of self-belief. To have self-belief is to have faith and confidence in one's self, and all that you believe about yourself is positive and empowering. Self-belief is about being certain in your abilities and judgements whilst believing in your own worth. And having self-belief provides you with a sound basis and strong structural framework for success. To have self-belief is invaluable and most important for a stress- and distress-free life. Self-belief is vital for your physical, emotional, and mental well-being.

Renowned author Louise Hay succinctly points out her perspective on self-belief, sharing her philosophy in her book *You Can Heal Your Life*:

> We are each 100% responsible for all of our experiences. Every thought we think is creating our future. The point of power is always in the present moment. Everyone suffers from self-hatred and guilt. The bottom line for everyone is, "I'm not good

enough." It's only a thought, and a thought can be changed. Self approval and self-acceptance in the now is the key to positive changes. We create every so-called illness in our body.

Her insight into the necessity for self-belief clearly identifies it as impacting not only your physical well-being, but also your entire life experience. Your self-perception may have originated from the past; however, it is what you believe about yourself now that matters. And that belief has been formulated in your mind through your thoughts. And the good news is, you can change your thoughts. Herein is a powerful insight with which to facilitate change.

The spiritual text *A Course in Miracles* further explains the overriding power of self-belief:

> It is hard to recognise that thought and belief combined into a power surge that can literally move mountains. It appears at first glance that to believe such a power about yourself is arrogant, but that is not the real reason you do not believe it. You prefer to believe that your thoughts cannot exert real influence because you are actually afraid of them.

So you are afraid to look within for fear of discovering that your fears and illusions may be real, believing them to be so. However, your fear is more likely that of your true power. Nevertheless, it is important to look within, to your thoughts and beliefs, for they are what we believe them to be. And it is where you comprehend your world and create the reality of your self within that world. Often you may think the law of attraction is in play, yet actually you are recreating your thought beliefs and validating them.

It is also empowering to know where your particular level of beliefs about yourself originated. Self-knowledge is gained from the time you enter this world as a baby. Your identity in this new lifetime was yet to be fully determined, but the process began immediately. Children have no knowledge of the perception of other people's own self-beliefs and how that influences their own sense of self. It is essential for children to have a strong positive role model, as this then determines their ability to navigate their life experience successfully.

Much of what you accept as your belief system has been imposed upon you through the direct or indirect influence of others. These influences include the people around you, your cultural background, the community in which you live, society as a whole, your ancestral heritage, and something called the collective consciousness and unconsciousness. At each and every stage of your life, these are the many and varied influences contributing to your perception of self. This, in turn, impacts your level of self-belief. Belief systems about your self are formulated by outside influences. These beliefs are then mostly considered true. But are they?

You now know the stimuli for your beliefs originated in the world around and outside of yourself. Nonetheless, those outside of yourself did not make you believe. You formulated your beliefs yourself, for various reasons, within your own mind. What you think in each moment regarding your life experiences creates your reality. You make a judgement of what you see, hear, and feel from your particular perspective, creating a belief around that experience. You then file that in your subconscious mind, where it delegates all other similar experiences to the same belief system.

Belief and Faith

Belief is also about having faith. Faith in self is having self-belief. How do you gain this faith when it has been lost (or never existed)? You gain faith firstly by knowing who you truly are. Trusting the innate goodness of yourself is also important in gaining faith in yourself. Faith in yourself naturally rises when you know who you truly are rather than believing in who you are not.

What was learnt can be unlearnt, and what was thought can be changed by learning anew. It is important to verify the validity of beliefs, for many are false. Many self-beliefs, particularly negative ones, are invalid. In fact, from a metaphysical view, there is evidence only for self-belief as truth.

To reconnect with the truth of self, who you truly are, you only need to look within. Looking within refers to discovering the thought processes and belief systems you possess. Everyone can do this to some extent by themselves. You can consciously observe the thoughts you have of the world outside of yourself. You also need to monitor the thoughts, judgements, and prejudices of others, acknowledging what you make of what you see and experience. Nevertheless, it is more difficult to analyse that which is in your subconscious or unconscious mind. Seeking the help of a professional to support you in this process is also very beneficial.

Self-Help for Self-Belief

In my work with clients, no matter what the complaint, the underlying issue is always a poor sense of self. When working with my students, all my teachings are based upon the central theme of the self and the value of self-belief. This is done in particular from the metaphysical perspective of the God self. With both students and clients, I have a structure that I work to, leading them from self-doubt to self-love.

These are the stages I work through to bring each client to self-belief through self-love:

1) Discover. What is the issue? How did this situation occur and why?

2) Clarify. The belief systems that has been formed regarding their situation and around others involve (if any) and their self.

3) Authenticate. To discover in truth if their beliefs around their issue and themselves are valid.

4) Expose. Exploring their conscious belief systems, in thought, word, and deed, makes it possible to uncover the unconscious belief systems.

5) Rectify. Replace the false and illusionary belief systems with the truth.

6) Enable. The aim is always to reach the place where clients not only know that they have everything they need within them, but they now also have tools and strategies with which to successfully self-analyse for self-mastery.

Some of the tools and strategies that I find helpful to give to clients include affirmations, prayers, meditation, specific personal action tasks, new mindset thinking, word meaning clarification, new perception understanding, recognition of falsehoods and illusions, and true self (God self) recognition.

You have had your beliefs for so long that you may, for various reasons, find it problematic to let go of your negative thought patterns. The process of letting go is just changing a negative thought by releasing the false belief and replacing it with the truth. Use this eight-stage process if you find it difficult to let go:

1) Identify the false belief and determine why it is false.

2) Observe that the belief has no value in your life, is no longer valid, or is actually destructive.

3) Discover if the original belief may have been based on a misinterpretation and therefore is an illusion.

4) Acknowledge evidence of and benefit for an alternative belief.

5) Recognise the truth of the new belief or thought.

6) Choose to release the old false belief by letting it go.

7) Replace the old belief with the truth, establishing a new belief around the situation, event, or person.

8) Accept the truth, knowing it to be true.

You will discover that no matter where, when, or how your beliefs were formulated, they still exist in the now (or present moment) for you. It is in this now moment that they need to be examined to verify their validity. And it is in the now moment that you can choose to release (or retain) your beliefs. It is important that you believe you can change your disempowering beliefs through the power of choice and the power of your mind. The process can be done slowly or quickly; it is all up to you and what you believe.

Belief in Your True Self

Since my early days as a school teacher, I have been fascinated (and alarmed) by the lack of self-belief in my young students. Now in my work as a healer, counsellor, and adult educator, I still see a similar lack of self-belief. Many clients have little or no faith in themselves, not knowing their true value. Most recognise the beauty and value of others yet fail to accept it within themselves. Recognising and coming to know your own worth and value is the all-important first step towards building (or, perhaps more accurately, restoring) your true self. A healthy belief in self is not about ego. Rather, it is a return to your true self in love.

Making for Vibrational Alignment

Beliefs are initiated in thought: what you think about what you witnessed and experienced, and what you made it mean. You create meaning in your world in the power of your thoughts. Even more importantly, these thoughts dictate your beliefs about yourself having an impacting on your level of self-belief. Not all beliefs are valid, and the self you have made in your mind is rarely legitimate. You may have also accepted the belief systems of others as truth, often without question. It is only when your life is not what you want it to be or is in breakdown that you begin to question why. Why are you *attracting* what you have experienced into your life?

If you are not getting what you want, there is a block within you. That block is often a false belief that you need to work at to let go of, before attraction can occur. What is being attracted to yourself is what you believe in. In that frame of belief, you vibrate, creating an energy field which is magnetised to attract more of what you are believing in. To get what you want (that is, different from what you have), you need to think differently about what you want. This is not always easy; sometimes, it is beneficial to learn, be guided, seek help and support in changing your mindset. Changing your mindset thereby changes your physical energy vibration to that which you would prefer to attract into your life.

To generate change in yourself, it is important to uncover the thoughts you have about your self, both positive and negative. That is where the self-belief is created (or miscreated). It is also crucial to know how these beliefs were formed and the original influencers of these beliefs. These original influencers of the infant include parents, siblings, immediate family, and friends. The collective consciousness also influences you, providing another level of self-awareness that adds to (or diminishes) self-esteem. In a world filled with fear, wars, and disasters, there seems to be more evidence for lack of self-belief than belief in the goodness of self and others.

When each self-sabotaging conviction is replaced with your true self, your self-connection and self-esteem will be uncovered and develop positively.

Do you pay attention to your thoughts to discover your beliefs? They are the true indicators of what you are attracting into your life. The mind is where you formulate your ongoing thought patterns. Will wanting financial abundance manifest into reality if you believe, for some reason, that there is not enough wealth in the world to go around? What you think and believe in is your perceived reality, a reality/illusion created from your beliefs. Whether there is truth in your belief or not, it is enough that you believe in it. Hence, it is important to discover your many beliefs and then test them to discover their validity in truth and their value to you in your life.

"The understanding usually developed is nothing more than a 'belief' which means nothing at all. The only belief that is of any value to anyone is a belief that has been put to the test and demonstrated to be a fact; then it's no longer a belief but has a living Truth."

—Charles F. Haanel

Being in vibrational alignment is to believe in and for yourself that which you wish to attract.

Channelled Insight

What is it that you believe, my child:

A mountain is a molehill,

or a molehill to be a mountain?

Believing it to be does not make it so,

although we allow you to make it so.

Believe what you will,

yet the truth will never change.

You are at one with all,

perfect in name and nature.

Your beliefs, ever contrary,

will never make the otherwise,

will never make the other wise.

Affirmation Statements

- I lovingly embrace joyful life experiences.

- I am shedding my excess weight.

- I have an abundance of all that I need and want.

- I am open and accepting to more of what I desire into my life.

- I have abundance in all aspects of my life.

- I value, love, and embrace financial abundance.

- I embrace all the positive aspects of my life.

- I choose to be happy. I deserve to be happy.

Follow-Up Tasks

Write out the beliefs you have about

- your family,

- your friendships,

- life in general,

- society,

- religion,

- money,

- work, and

- yourself.

Note whether they are still relevant in your life or not.

CHAPTER 4

The Law of Cause and Effect

The Law that Partners with the Law of Attraction

Nothing happens without there first being a cause

"Life without a cause is life without an effect." —Paulo Coelho

Oxford Dictionary

Cause a) thing that produces an effect, **b)** person or thing that occasions or produces something, **c)** reason or motive.

Effect result or consequence of an action etc.

Law Definition

Every outcome or effect, whether it is an event, situation, person, or happening, had a beginning or point of origin.

The Law

Every situation, event, or happening first had an initial cause: a beginning point, an originating moment. That which initiated and set into motion what eventually occurred is often overlooked (or even ignored). Time after time, in wanting to relieve an undesired occurrence, the focus is on what happened and reacting to it, rather than why it happened. Focusing on why a situation occurred will give you a better insight in resolving any issues and gain better information for a future better outcome.

When you experience an event, situation, or person who affects you, consciously or unconsciously, you immediately put a meaning to it. *You* make it mean something. In fact, everything that you observe and experience has some effect on you. That effect may be positive, or it may be negative: good or bad. If the experience was positive, you will in future associate all like experiences by having a similar positive reaction. If you had a negative experience, you will more likely associate any like encounter by having a similarly negative response.

Whether the experience was visual, physical, or emotional, your resultant emotional connection to the experience is stored in your subconscious memory bank. This memory deposit is then ever ready for a withdrawal, a recall of that same memory, if and when a seemingly similar situation arises. Although no two situations are exactly alike, your subconscious brain relays a message to your body that it is the same. Then the physical, psychological, and emotional parts of your body go into protection mode. It protects, seemingly, the memory from the past by responding to the situation in the same way as you have done in the past. All the while, the unconscious mind is unaware and does not recognise that no two situations are exactly alike; and this new situation needs to be reacted to differently. You are essentially on autopilot, reacting rather than reasoning, working from the unconscious mind rather than being consciously aware. All this happens in seconds of your experiencing, responding from your earlier learnt experience.

Whether you initiated what happened or not, your subconscious mind (through your conscious awareness) puts a meaning to the experience and holds it there forever. Then it matches each like experience, believing it to be the same, sending messages to the brain to act and react in the way you first responded. Everything is done unconsciously, in unawareness, although you believe you are fully aware and in charge of every situation and interaction. This does not need to be the case. Being aware of how your unconscious or subconscious mind works is the first step in self-mastery.

You are the cause of everything that affects you.

There is an outcome to every thought, word, and deed that affects your life one way or another. Some outcomes are positive, some negative. Every situation, event, or happening first had an initial thought cause in your mind. Often in wanting to relieve an undesired or painful occurrence all you have time for is to react to a situation, event, or person. You may not have time to discover the reason you find yourself in that situation, which may be negative or challenging. Even if you try, you may not be given all the information necessary to know the initial cause of the situation or event, particularly if you are not the cause.

You tend to justify your actions rather than look for a cause for your actions (or the actions of others). You rarely look for the cause of something that was said or something that happened that impacted your life. If you do, you often make a judgement as to the cause. And in that judgement, you are more likely to make yourself wrong, for your words or deeds. Often you do this without all the facts. Perhaps the belief in your intuition or gut feeling is enough evidence of truth, all the while little realising that you are actually making an emotional judgement rather than being intuitive. That is not to say that intuition is not real and useful, only that it can be misinterpreted.

If someone upsets you, you may feel quite rightly that their words are inappropriate. You never look to what is behind the words that are said or why. You may consider the question but rarely seek to find the true answer, rather spending time to interpret the mind of another. This interpretation from your mind reading another's is open to mistakes and misunderstandings. Neither do you look to what it is that triggered the hurt within you. It is more likely that you believe the other person made you feel bad or negative because of what was said or done. What precipitated the response in you?

Or you may blame yourself for the person treating you badly. You may not realise the person is in a negative place, a place that has nothing to do with you. You are not the cause of their rage. They are more likely misdirecting the cause of their upset onto you. This happens frequently. If everyone looked to the original cause of their upset, it would be possible to overcome (or at least clear up) whatever is troubling them. This is the ideal, rather than what is happening in most people's lives.

It is mostly fear that dictates your unwillingness to look at the cause of what upsets you. There in itself is an effect: fear. Your thoughts have created the fear. The fear of making yourself wrong, not being good enough or worthwhile, is often the cause of being fearful. More often than not, others are also in fear. Many actions, in word or deed, are based in fear. You may have never considered whether the fear was learnt, instilled, or created. All the while, you escape challenging the root of the fears in thought. For many people, challenging the fear gives rise to even more fear. All the while, you are creating (and recreating) fearful effect after effect, never addressing the cause of your fears.

You may be fearful of looking at the cause of your actions or words. You may believe some misfortune you've had to endure to be caused by another person (or life in general). Yet all the while, deep down, you are afraid, for you unconsciously have already blamed yourself. So you avoid looking for a cause of your own actions, fearful the examination will show you to be the cause. This cause, fault, or blame of any action must be someone. And if that cause is bad, you don't want that someone to be you (and understandably so).

You never consider that perhaps there is no wrong or right. How can that be? You have been taught all your life what is right and what is wrong. You were taught to judge: judging everything as wrong or right, appropriate or inappropriate. Over time, people began judging each other rather than their actions, judging the person rather than judging the action. There are so many reasons as to why people behave in a particular way. We all look at others through our own lenses, our own viewpoint. This then makes it difficult to discover the true cause for an action of another. There are so many variables as to why people behave in certain ways and why events happen.

Others create the effects you see. If their actions affect you, it will benefit you to look at why their actions had an effect on you. You are not the cause of their actions. However, how you view, respond, and interpret what you hear or see of another is your responsibility. You are then the cause of that response, as it is having an effect on you. This is often called having your buttons pressed. While you believe this is possible, the underlying thought system is that you have no control over what another is doing. What if in reality, you are the one pressing your own button as a response to something that is upsetting you?

When my clients regard a situation that has had an effect on them, I say that if someone presses their button, that it is their problem to solve. They need to look at themselves as to why that had an effect on them. What is it that caused them to react to a situation? What is it within them that created that effect? If you can answer these questions, you will begin to take back control of your life. Look to find the cause by first understanding the thought that led you to have that reaction. You then have an insight as to why it had an effect on you. To find peace of mind, where there are no negative effects, all you need is to change your thoughts from negative to positive.

Sometimes, for change to occur, you may need help with a different insight or a different way of thinking. You can do this on your own or with the help of a professional who specialises in the field of mind work. In this scenario, you are the one in control. You can choose the emotional or mental reaction to what is said or done to you. You may not agree with another's behaviour; however, you do not need to let it affect you negatively. You are then choosing to be in control, controlling your response to the situation rather than allowing it to affect you. You are then in your power.

When you look to better understand a person's action, an event, or a situation, you may make assumptions as to the cause. Unless you have all the information, you cannot make a correct judgement call. In looking for why something happened, real positive progress can be actioned in your life. The underlying cause in every effect and every outcome will reveal the reason for a particular action or behaviour of others (and even of yourself). If you have experienced a negative emotion, situation, or interaction, discovering the cause can help you understand how to better navigate your personal experiences. You can do this by resolving the effect on yourself by dealing appropriately with the initial cause.

Being aware of the cause of your life experiences gives you the key information to create the life of your dreams. It all depends on the actions you take, beginning with your thought actions. These, then, are the vibrations that attract to you like vibrations. This is how the law of cause and effect partners with the law of attraction.

The old saying Buddhist saying, "Be careful what you think," seems to hold true.

It's a case of input/output. How often have you heard "Change your thought and you change your world" (Norman Vincent Peale)?

Sometimes, this quote is misunderstood as "Changing your mind will bring about change in another." What truly happens is that the change happens in how you see the world around you, not because anything has changed (apart from your interpretation of what is). Your changing mindset can help influence change in another. This, then, is about another universal law called the law of allowing: allowing others to be as they are and not how you want them to be. We all want to be allowed to be ourselves. You may only begin to judge because you feel you are being judged. Sometime, somehow, someone needs to put an end to causing that which affects you negatively. Why not begin with yourself, for that is truly the only place where a difference will occur?

You are not the cause of everything you experience.

If someone threw a ball, and you saw who threw it and watched the direction of that ball, what would you see? What would you think? What would you make it all mean? What do you make it mean as you read this? You may notice the speed and velocity of the throw and subsequent path of the ball. You may even notice the expression and stance of the thrower. You may have noticed the direction in which the ball was aimed. Once the ball left the hand of the thrower, it was now out of their control. All was dependant on the throw. The ball may have gone a short or long distance. It may bounce, miss, or hit an object in its path. It may achieve the aim of the thrower or not. All the while you watch, you know, consciously or unconsciously, you had no influence on the action taken by another. Many factors impact the end result of the initial throw: the force of the throw, the size and mass of the ball, the ability and intent of the thrower.

In this simple scenario, did the observer do anything other than observe? Did the mere act of observation have any impact on the movement of the ball? Never in all this would you consider you had any bearing on the outcome of the ball's throw.

If a ball rolled by you or you saw it fly through the air, would you consider you were the cause of that ball's movement? Would you think you attracted that ball to yourself? Unfortunately, many who have heard of the law of attraction believe they attract everything which comes into their pathway. Although you did see the movement of the ball, the reality is, no attraction occurred. What was in play here was the universal law of cause and effect. Why is it, then, that we are being told that everything we see we attracted to ourselves? Some people believe this to be the case.

You did not attract that experience to yourself. It was already in play; you happened to be having the experience as an observer. The choice was yours to continue to observe or not. If you stayed to observe, you had an experience. Everything is an experience, and with each experience, you learn, making it mean something, and then you store it in your memory. What is helpful to consider is the effect the experience has had on you and know that you are responsible for that effect. Whether you enjoyed the experience, found it annoying, or of no consequence, this is your response to what you observed. The thrower of the ball is not the cause of what you observed and made it mean.

How you're affected is dependant on a number of variables. If you could come to the experience with a blank mind, then you may not have an emotional response while viewing the ball being thrown. However, you have had a lifetime of previous experiences: a knowledge of balls and people who throw balls. You are likely to have thoughts, opinions, and possibly even emotional responses to this event based on your biases of balls and people who throw them. You just have to watch a crowd at a sports event to see the effect the game has on their emotion and sensibilities.

More often than not, this is how we live our lives. You are unconsciously paying attention to what is unfolding in the world around you, wondering how to respond. In whichever way you do respond to an event, person, or situation, you rarely look at the cause of what you encountered. You more often than not merely react to the situation, person, or event.

A young child's first experience of a ball is much the same as people who have never seen a ball before. Once they see how it came to move and recognised the cause of the movement, they too wish to have a go. They then can be the cause for the effect of experiencing playing with a ball. In having that experience, they learn how the throw impacts movement, direction, speed, and landing of the ball. The child learns through that experience.

You too learn how to navigate through your life in a similar fashion. Any experience that is new, you learnt from the world around you, consciously or unconsciously. If you interpret the lesson as a positive or negative, you know now you are likely to categorise all similar experiences as the same. Then the unconscious mind goes into autopilot and responds as it did once before, even though the two occurrences are not the same. If your focus is on the law of attraction, then it is more likely you will believe you have attracted that into your life rather than it being the law of cause and effect. Perhaps it's just a lesson you need to learn as to why something is having an effect on you, rather than making yourself feel wrong and bad. A life lesson in itself is not good or bad. It is just a lesson, a learning exercise, a device or learning tool.

Partnering with the Law of Attraction

You are the cause of your life, knowingly or unknowingly. The good news is, you are not the cause of anyone else's life. The best news is, you are the cause of your life. Knowing how the law of cause and effect works universally can help you to take further action to elicit the effect of the life you choose to have. In other words, you can choose the thought you have, the actions you take, the friendships you keep, and the situations you wish to have. You have the free will to do so. Firstly, you need to decide on your desired outcome. How do you want your life to be? Then you need to know the actions to take to achieve that desired outcome. Which appropriate action will affect the result you choose to experience? This is the beginning of you attracting to yourself the life of your choosing. And you can do this better by knowing the law of cause and effect.

The effects of how your life looks is first germinated in your mind. In other words, the Cause is always a thought, in the millions of thoughts in your mind and the myriad thoughts around that original thought.

How you see your life and interpret it, creating other like thoughts and focusing on them, is how you cause the life experiences you choose for yourself.

You are the creative force of your life experiences. You are the architect.

You are the cause of how you see the world around or outside of you.

Are you the cause of it all? This is a question that I am intrigued with and needs to be understood more fully.

Once you understand this, you have the power to create the life of your dreams and desires. Sound easy? Well, yes and no. It's up to you. It's all up to you. You have created how you see your life up until now and will continue to do so. The question is, will you do it in awareness or unawareness (consciously or unconsciously)? Ego mind is the unconscious creator and can only recreate past thoughts. Taking back control and becoming a conscious creator, you can let go of the past thought patterns. You're un-creating (so to speak) and creating anew that which you truly want and desire from a mind place that you can relate to and understand to create from. By and through conscious cocreating with universal intelligence, you align your mind and thoughts with its vibration to then attract that which is for your highest good. The universal mind will always deliver that which you desire, even the lessons you need to have to get what you want.

You (the effect) are the Manifestation of Universal Mind Thought Cause.

Cause Vibration Manifestation

Everything is a vibration of each aspect of the created. All vibrational energy has an effect on us, as well as on others, be it positive or negative. Looking to the cause of that vibration will help you recognise what you can change to effect a better outcome for yourself and your life. Once you recognise the cause of the events in your life, you are able to take control and change your life more purposely and purposefully.

Your human nature tends to justify your actions rather than look to the cause of your actions. This sometimes is from a place of unawareness or fear. Fear dictates your unwillingness to look for the cause of your life experiences, particularly if they are considered to be problems. In unawareness, you don't have the tools to address the cause, and you continue the fear or "making yourself wrong" cycle. By addressing the cause of any fear or doubt, you have the key to unlock the root of any problem you find yourself in. Therein is your power: the power to overcome any doubt or fear illusion.

You can choose to take responsibility for the life experience or not. Being aware of your ability to choose your experiences enables you to continue that life experience in empowered awareness. Blame, judgement, resentment, and fear are all detrimental to a joyful and joy-filled experience. Moving past fear- and ego-based thought systems is your hurdle, and the final challenge, as you embrace your reawakening.

Others also create the effects you see. If they and their actions affect you, you need to look at what caused there to be an effect on you. You are not the cause of their situation. However, how you view, interpret, and respond to any given situation or person is your responsibility. You are then the cause of it (or them) having an effect on you.

For example, if someone said something that immediately pressed your buttons, so to speak, the cause of that reaction is within you. You are not the cause of their bad mood or insensitive words, even if they accuse you of being the cause. However, if (the effect) response on you is either emotionally or mentally negative (or positive), then the cause is within you and your mindset. In other words, something within you caused you to be affected by the remark rather than your friend being the cause of your upset. Just as you are not the cause of their bad mood (or even their positive mood), they are not the cause of your response to their behaviour. You can affect someone else to feel good (or not) around you, as they can have that effect on you. However, the *cause response* is always within you (or within them).

Look within yourself to find the cause of your actions and reactions. Come to understand your conscious and unconscious thought patterns, and you will begin to see why and how you attract. You will have gained an insight that can change your world. Then you can work to find a place within yourself for peace of mind.

You can choose to maintain a thought or change it.

For change to occur within, you need help to gain a different insight or a different way of thinking to access a better outcome for your better life. Remember it's a case of input/output.

The Empowering Sense of Responsibility

Knowing the law of cause and effect can cause you to be empowered. Why and how, you may ask? Knowing why something happens, knowing how it happens, and knowing who caused an event give you truth and insight.

If you are not the cause of a situation or event, you cannot be held responsible for the outcome, unless the outcome impacts you in some way. Needless to say, you are also not responsible of any impact to another. That is, unless you decide to interfere and add to the cause. If you discover you are the cause of a situation, you are then able to do something about it to effect a different outcome, if you so choose. Being the cause, you and only you can change the outcome if you wish to. However, at the same time, you are not responsible if what you did unintentionally affects another. Here, I clarify "unintentionally," as sometimes unconsciously, you may seem to cause unhappiness for another because they unconsciously recalling a past experience. You will not be able to effect a better outcome here, as you are not the cause of their upset; their own past experience is. If they are unaware of what they are remembering, they often will blame you for causing their upset.

Just as your mind can be in a negative or positive state, so too can the minds of others. Most often, you don't know the mind state others are in. Even the most spiritual or psychic people don't go around "reading" minds. When you act or react, you are often unaware of your mind space, be it negative or positive; as for others, you don't know if they are having difficulties. Few people willingly share their unconscious past experiences and life challenges with others. All you can do is the best you know how in any given situation and endeavour to learn from each. Blame and guilt are not your friends, for they will teach you nothing valuable, only further fear and judgement. Acknowledgement and reparation will free you from guilt and blame; they can open you up to learning how to live your life better and have a better life experience.

There is an effect to every thought, word, and deed that anyone puts out into the universe. All too often, people react to what has affected them rather than looking for the cause of the effect. Looking to the cause can action real, positive progress. The underlying cause in every effect will reveal the reasoning action. Some outcomes are positive, some negative.

What do you choose to attract into your life? What has already been attracted into your life? Knowing the reason why and the how in the law of cause and effect is of value, so you know how to align yourself, being the cause for that which you wish to attract to your life experience.

Channelled Insight

What caused you to be who you are, be where you are at, and do what you do?

Others, you would answer.

Others, you would believe is correct,

yet deep down within you, you are unsure of the process, the happening.

Often until it is in your mind too late.

It is never too late, to undo, to redo, to begin again.

We are here to let you know that what you acknowledge, what you fear is easily overcome and rectified.

You are not the cause of everything happening in this world, although you are responsible for all the good you do and all that you do in fear.

When one thing is done, know that it is over and a new day can be chosen to do more.

You do not need to repeat forever that which you have experienced.

Affirmation Statements

- I choose not to be negatively affected by another.

- I am now and always good enough.

- I am taking positive action in this situation.

- I am willing to learn for my personal growth.

- I take responsibility and learn positively for my growth and evolution.

- I listen to my higher self-wisdom before I take action.

- I take appropriate action for my success attraction.

Follow-Up Tasks

- When you see a resultant situation, begin to enquire how it began so as to have this particular outcome.

- If you find yourself responding to situations, see if you can consciously take an action with a particular result in your mind you wish to achieve.

- Think about the reasons you choose to do something.

- Pay attention to your thoughts. You have millions of bits of information that go through your brain. Not all of them become dominant or even semi-dominant thoughts. Pay attention to the ones you have a strong emotional reaction to, be it positive or negative. As you learn to recognise them, celebrate your positive thoughts and work to eliminate your negative thoughts by transcending to a positive mindset.

- Pay attention to the words you say. This is often easier to do than pay attention to the myriad thoughts within your mind. Always note the first thing you have said for it is the subconscious minds thought. Have you caught yourself saying, "Oh, that's not what I meant"? That is what you unconsciously meant. You most likely do not believe it yet your subconscious mind has not let go of it. This, then, is something you know you need to work to remove from your subconscious mind. You no longer consciously think that way yet the subconscious mind has not 'got it' yet.

- Pay attention to your actions. There is a reason for the saying, "Actions speak louder than words." Again if your actions do not align with your thoughts and words then you are out of alignment and this also impact your ability to attract that which you want into your life.

CHAPTER 5

The Law of Love

The Law that Propels the Law of Attraction to You

Total, Unconditional, Affectionate Acceptance

"Love the Lord your God with all your heart and with all your soul and with all your strength and with your entire mind and Love your neighbour as yourself." (Luke 10:27)

Oxford Dictionary

Love deep affection or fondness.

Law Definition

Unconditionally loving another regardless of what they do, how they are, or how they choose to live their life, particularly in relationship with others.

The Law of Attraction and Law of Love

Many have heard of the law of attraction, yet they are not fully aware of the law that powerfully propels for attraction creation: the law of love.

The law of love is the first, the highest, and the most powerful of universal laws. This law transcends all other laws, also helping to power other universal laws. It is a universal law, as opposed to a commandment.

> "If you are not getting as much from life as you want to, then examine the state of your enthusiasm."—Napoleon Hill

The universe does not judge and does not acknowledge judgements you make. It only responds to the passionate thought energy you are vibrating at. Any of your perceived negative mindsets appear as a desire for that is the message, or vibrational energy, you are emitting. This may be in response to your feelings about money, friendships, work, or even self-image. This is what the universe hears, and you then get more of what you are emanating, even if your passionate desire is for fewer of these experiences. Now that you know this, don't be concerned that you may inadvertently attract to yourself that which you no longer want to have n your life. Know that everything is a learning lesson, and if you have what you don't want in your life, all you need is to learn to love and love appropriately. If you wish to have that which you do want, you need to be passionate and love that which you do want. Love it. Love money, love your health, love your well-being, love your body, and so on. Love whatever you wish to manifest, and live it in the here and now.

> "Thought impregnated with love becomes invincible."—Charles F. Haanel

The law of love is the first and only universal law that is beyond all things universal, working for the highest good of all and at one with the Divine Source Love, a divine being infinitely loving and accepting each manifested creation unconditionally. The divine source sees no fault or error and makes no judgement on the perfectly created being that is you. In this deep sense of love, the divine gave us a garden of perfection called Eden, giving each the gift of free will to enjoy all that is therein. However, in the process of letting us play alone, without the divine, we got lost; we began to become delusional and to believe in a hell. The law of love is where we will once again find our way back home: back to our true nature. Are we not all looking to be loved and to love in its truest sense: unconditionally? Why is that so, if not for the fact that it is who we truly are: loving, created beings?

Considering the law of attraction, you are often encouraged to focus on your dreams and your desires so you can attract these dreams and desires into your life. Desire is all about love and loving the object that you want, that you desire (e.g., a relationship of your dreams, financial abundance, great health, long and happy life, etc.). Loving that which you want will propel it to you.

Loving purposely and powerfully propels to you that which you desire.

The Barriers to Positive Attraction

What happens when you are getting what you don't want? It may be not enough money, the wrong life partner, the wrong job, or any personal desire that is unfulfilled. It is then important to look at what it is that you're unconsciously focusing on. What are your thoughts or thought beliefs regarding these issues? Are the thoughts loving or fearful? The universe is only attuned to your strongest vibrational thought, be it love or fear. You may want to have financial abundance or meet the person of your dreams, but economic lack or nightmare partners always show up. Perhaps your desires for your self are unfulfilled. All that is in your subconscious (or perhaps even in your conscious awareness) is emanating from every cell of your body. Consciously or unconsciously, that is what you are putting your thought energy into. Even though it may not be what you want or chose consciously, you may not be aware that you have subconsciously accepted and keep validating the opposing thought, rather than your loving desire. At the same time, know that other laws are also involved with what is going on with you and your thoughts.

For financial abundance, you need to love money and all things connected to it.

Check your thoughts around money. Do you have any negative conditioning around money? Do you have any negative perceptions around money? Do you have any negative belief systems around money? If you do, then address them and find a way to transform your negative mindset to a positive one in relationship to money.

For good health, you need to believe it is possible at all times for you.

People who wish to lose weight, for instance, usually have a negative perception regarding their body image or a negative mindset impacting their body image. Loving your body, unconditionally, and not equating it to physical love is a beginning for positive self-transformation. You may have an aversion to exercise. For the well-being of your physical body, exercise is a great source of wellness. Learn to love it, even if it takes time. You may have an aversion to taking pills for your well-being. Some bodies need certain medications to chemically enhance and support physical wellness not knowing yet they have the power within to heal. Learn to love the creation of a support plan for your well-being when necessary (for your health rather than for dependence) until you grow to know you have within you all you need for healing through the power of your mind. Then in the passionate powerful use of your mind you can learn to as Louise Hay says *You Can Heal Life*.

For a great relationship, you need to develop a great relationship with yourself.

It is valuable to look to the qualities you seek in a partner to discover what kind of partner you wish to attract. Consider people who constantly attract partners who have issues. In discovering the qualities they want in a partner, they may first appear to be positive. However, they may add they want someone with a "bad boy" or "bad girl" personality, as all good: may seem to be too good. Yet this is the quality that is the key source of energy vibration attracting what is thought to be wanted (but in actuality is not). Choosing a rebellious personality type may be due to a missed understanding about noncompliance and being your own person. They make choices that sometimes are not popularly liked but the best for you; this is not being bad or good. It is just the best choice for you. Rebellion is not agreeing; it is going against others for the sake of it. Recognising your right to choose is not rebellious, as your shift in mindset can then bring on a different, more positive attraction.

For a wonderful life experience, you need to learn to love yourself.

Fear, in particular fear of rejection, often holds you back in many areas of your life, personally and professionally. Your fear of not being liked, not being accepted, not being valued are some of the visions of rejection. You are so blinded by your fears that you don't see that it is your own lack of self-love that is the cause of many of them.

When you begin to recognise your self-worth, accepting all aspects of your human self lovingly, without judgement and unconditionally, you will begin to experience heaven on earth. Seeing beyond the human into your spiritual nature, you will undeniably see that there is a very likeable (and even lovable) being that is called you. It is then that you will find joy, success, and happiness in your personal and professional life.

Check the negative conversations that are in your mind, that are your thoughts, thoughts that disempower you. Know that many of these thoughts are just opinions, often imposed by others, that have become beliefs (and false ones, at that). They do not come from a place of love and are more likely fear-based.

The law of love is the most powerful law of the universe.

Acknowledge what you love and where you are being loving:

- I love my family and enjoy special time with them.

- I value my friends and love spending fun times with each of them.

- I love my work and get great satisfaction from it.

- I have a wonderfully special loving relationship with my partner and always will.

- I value and love who I am and continue to grow into an even more loving being.

You may be able to add to this list of loving thoughts and actions you make.

This is a powerful acknowledgement of who you are in this time and space. How often have you found faults and flaws in your human self? This can be valuable, inasmuch as you know what to improve on, rather than something to admonish yourself for. However, it is even more valuable (and certainly more important) to acknowledge the good you have done and the personal growth you have achieved. These positive thought vibrations allow for more positive thoughts to enter your mind space for further positive growth. In doing so, you are giving yourself the loving acknowledgement of what you have achieved, rather than only seeing what you have not. A negative and admonishing thought system gives you less of what you want, rather than building on what you have achieved. When you begin to give yourself acknowledgement, which is loving recognition, you'll be surprised to discover there is more to given yourself credit for. And in that vibration, you will attract more of all that is wonderful and desirable coming into your life.

"Neither a lofty degree of intelligence nor imagination
nor both together go to the making of genius.
Love, love, love, that is the soul of genius."

—Wolfgang Amadeus Mozart

The Universe Created All in Love

When the notion of love is considered, it is usually in a human romantic context, although the first form of love we all experience is from our parents. Over time, you then come to experience friendship love, along with romantic love and love for material things. All of these pale in the sight of pure, unconditional love. You may have experienced this love firstly from your parents, some from friends, or even from a love partner. However, human love is often filled with conditions, although at times unintentionally, as ego comes into play.

The universal law of love, based on divine love, is not the concept of human love, rather the highest form of love, which is totally unconditional, for it is given from the divine source mind and not from the mind of ego. Divine Source Love knows no fear, sees no evil, hears no evil, and most importantly does not judge. Contrary to some other beliefs, the divine mind sees only the perfection it created, knowing it cannot miscreate itself or make the false real. For a time, the created you may live in the false illusion you have made that seems real, but you cannot stay there forever. The time for all illusions and delusions will disappear, and you will come to see truth and reality in love.

Loving you unconditionally, the universal intelligence of the divine source mind delivers to you that which its vibration acknowledges you love. If you fear more than love the good in your life, your fears will manifest. Your fears are delivered to you by the universe. It responds to your strongest vibration, sending you your like vibration. You often don't realise you are sending your fear thoughts out into the universe. You get what you want, even though you believe you don't want it. The universe only responds to your passionate plea, although the plea may be for that which you don't want. However, loving you unconditionally, the universe also know that you will eventually learn freely, for you have free will, that which you want to love more than you fear it. Divine Source Love, in loving you, is constantly working to move heaven and earth for your eventual return to your loving, empowered self. Why are you reading this, if not to find a way back: back to the truth of you, back to the loving of you?

Reconnecting to Divine Source Love

Meditating on nothing is meditating on "no-thingness," so that your thoughts for your highest good can come to you. You who are in fear, who doubt, and who are disillusioned don't realise how powerful you are; your unconscious intent may be stronger than your conscious intent. It then appears to the universe as a want or a desire. Universal intelligence is not thinking like a human being. Its only thoughts are of pure love and bringing to you that which you are vibrating. It is not a judging mechanism and is not judging what is good or not good for you. Also, it is not judging you for your choices. When in a state of no-thingness, leaving the universal law of love to work on its own, your highest good is always delivered to you. This doesn't mean you cannot ask for what you want. You may not know that something else is better for you; you may even be consciously aware that something else could be better for you but you don't know what it is or could be. There are times when just being open to what the universe sends you in love may surprise and delight you.

You are a precious jewel in the crown of royalty. You have been created in love by the source of divine love. You exist because you were conceived in loving thought. You are the manifested reality of Divine Source Love thought.

Is this not enough evidence of your worth? God does not make mistakes. God made perfect all that is physically contained in the world you live in: the sky, the sea, the birds, the trees, and the whole universe. Regardless of how you believe it was created, it was created by a source greater than any individual human being. This source was originally called God. I refer to it as Divine Source, as the source of all that is divine in nature. God made you perfectly too. You are equal to any of these creations (if not more so), and if you can see the good and the beauty in another, why do you believe you are less than? Your belief is false. You are perfect. Believing otherwise will not override the truth. You may play small, for you are free to do so, but it doesn't change the fact that you have power within you.

Be the Light of Love

Some people have lost their way and wandered off course so far they believe they are bad, wrong, and downright evil, so they live into that reality. They have made it to be so, and so it is for them. Others believe evil exists, so they find it in another, seeing what they want to see. And acts of evil are available for us to see, there is no doubt. Why they exist is a question we are not yet able to answer. As stated in chapter 5, what you believe, you see and create from a power base of your own greatness, a power that comes from your creator; it can be used to harm or heal, build or destroy.

What can you achieve if you take up your royal heritage, accept the perfection of your creation, and live in that vibration? Live. Love. Not an ego or egocentric love, nor a false sense of denying your heritage of greatness, but truly embracing it. Why not love unconditionally, as so often you are able to love others? Give that unconditional loving to yourself. Do not judge yourself harshly, believing you are worth less than another, that you are unworthy. Deny not your royal blood, and live with dignity and integrity, worthy of who you truly are. Recognise and acknowledge other selves at one with you in spirit.

So how can you live in a world that may wish to deny this heritage? Again, love is the answer. Certainly not in the human ego: questioning and filled with doubt and scepticism. Question, yes, and verify for yourself what you choose to believe and live by.

It is not for anyone to change or conflict with another's free will. Rather, be the light that guides them back home to their true nature. Know that their eyes (ears and mind) may be blinded to the light. But in time, they will become accustomed to it and to yours. So keep shining. Keep being. They have not journeyed the road you are on. Know that spirit will guide them back home, as this is inevitable for us all.

You have come to share a physical experience in human form, to grow, to evolve and to be. The time has come when you no longer want or need the negative, challenging experiences of your life. You will become aware that there must be something better than pain, fear, judgement, and a lack of true love. This is your higher mind, your higher self, calling you back to love, calling you back to who you truly are.

What would it be like if you could continue this physical experience, in awareness of the spirit of your true self? There comes a time when we are all ready for this. I know you are ready because you are reading this book. You were drawn to it for one reason or another, for it is your time, your time to live a more rewarding spirit- and joy-filled human experience.

Live in love. Live in the joy of your life.

You may ask how can I, when I see misery that surrounds the world I live in? The answer is as simple as you believe it to be complex. What do you choose to focus your love on? When you see with eyes of love (not romanticised love), you will gain insights that your human brain will not comprehend. So often, we try to understand with our human brain that which is beyond human understanding. To understand that which is beyond the physical, you need to connect with your higher mind, the mind connected to the divine source love. The mind of spirit has a knowing beyond the physical; it is universal and of the universe.

Over time, as you connect more and more with your higher spiritual self, universal understanding will become clearer. Meditation and prayer are two great ways to connect with your higher mind and spirit. If, for any reason, you are not able to do so, seek out a spirit-filled light worker who can light the way for you. This is not about blindly accepting all in love. Rather, it is acknowledging where or when the loveless appears, and unconditionally loving all in truth. Perhaps that true loving will be in the form of forgiveness, compassion, tolerance, understanding, and willingness to move past fear, judgement, and blame, not only of others but also of yourself.

Nonacceptance of a loveless act does not mean that you don't love unconditionally the person who is being unloving, perhaps even destructively so. Know that if the person knew better, loved and respected themselves better, they more likely would have made a better choice for themselves and their life.

In a state of fear, nothing is possible. In a state of love, everything is possible.

The Power of Loving Thankfulness

Giving thanks to the Divine Source of all is the same as giving thanks to anyone who gives you a gift of any kind. Divine Source has given you life, through the breath, the energy, of itself.

You have been given this life experience, within a beautiful world of abundance, filled with wondrous beings to share it all with. You have a lot to be grateful for, and yet you want and ask for more. This is okay, for the divine source's supply is endless, and it is happy to give. Showing gratitude acknowledges what you have and what you are thankful for. And like a generous parent, the divine source, through the law of love, hears your joy in your thanks and immediately gives you more of what has given you pleasure. So if you want more money in your life, be grateful for the money you have. If you want the partner of your dreams, be thankful for the partner the universe is sending to you. If you want a healthier or slimmer body, be grateful for the functioning body you do have. And in your gratitude, you are acknowledging your love of these gifts. Love money, not from an ego perspective but a spiritual one. Acknowledge the qualities you love in a dream partner. And yes, love your body; it is one of the most wonderful gifts given you to navigate this human experience.

When you focus on the negative, the divine source does not deny you that wish, either. The divine spirit of all does not recognise any negativity, only what you are giving your powerful thoughts to. Remember: It does not judge and fulfils your request, supplying you with what you are focusing on, be it intentionally or unintentionally.

Be that which you want to have in your life. Be happy and loving in the knowledge that all you want is being delivered to you in love and divine timing.

Love and loving self is the key to all your successes in life, not only personal success but also professional success. When you love yourself from the pure essence of unconditional love, you have self-confidence, self-esteem, and self-belief. You then no longer have a need to be fearful of others or be ego driven for your successes in life. The joy of love and loving will bring with it its own joyous rewards, more often than not beyond your wildest dreams.

Love that which you want. Then love will powerfully propel and attract to you all that you desire.

Channelled Insight

There are no laws in a world that does not need to be governed, where everything is love and loved, where no games need to be played, just pleasure to be had: the joy of being.

You play, and rules are needed to govern that the game be fair. A watchful eye is always upon you. The universe has been designed as a safe playpen, a safe learning environment for the children who play within it.

You do not realise you're playing; you don't realise the game. Learn as you go; everything is set in play for you to do so. These you call laws; we call them learning curves. You will be aware or not. But you will eventually see the game for what it is.

Know throughout the process that you are loved; you are guided, protected, and safe.

What you've come here to learn, you will ultimately discover.

When you are ready, you will know. When you learn, you will know. We are here at your disposal, at your bequest. For the moment, you may not remember, but remember you will. And the wanting is there, ready to be seen, ready to be acknowledged; knowing yourself as no other, loving yourself as no other, for there is no other.

Laws are there to revert any hurt. They explain the working of the universe and how it has been made for your benefit, for your learning. Choose to learn or not. In not choosing, you choose.

Wisdom comes in many forms.

The wise recognise, see.

The ignorant still gain sight.

The arrogant will forever be blind

The laws were made in love, for love and out of love, until you come back to love, no longer needing any law but love.

Affirmation Statements

- I love and accept myself just as I am.

- I love who I truly am.

- I love unconditionally.

- I am growing in self-love, self-acceptance, and self-belief.

- I give love to myself first; I have more of myself to give.

- I love and approve of myself, for I am the miracle of my life.

- I seek to find what to love in every experience, event, and person, particularly myself.

Follow-Up Tasks

- Acknowledge yourself whenever you do something you are proud of.

- List the things about yourself you are grateful for.

- Forgive yourself whenever you feel you've erred, and look for the learning lesson in the experience.

- As yourself "What do I want or need?" in each challenging or demanding situation you find yourself in.

- Seek to learn more about yourself and how your mind operates.

- Seek the support of a metaphysical practitioner specialising in self-actualisation to grow your self-awareness, self-esteem, and self-belief. Someone outside of yourself can intuitively reflect back to you your higher self.

CHAPTER 6

The Law of Mind

The First Point of Contact for Attraction

"The unchanging always waking spiritual law by which whatever we idealize and visualize materializes."—Charles F. Haanel

Oxford Dictionary

Mind Seat of consciousness, thought, volition, and feeling.

Law Definition

The mind houses thought, and all thought has manifested reality potential.

> "Problems cannot be solved with the same
> mind set that created them."
>
> —Albert Einstein

The Law of Mind

The mind is your creative powerhouse. The mind is not discerning. It does not acknowledge good or bad, negative or positive, or any other forms of duality. It acknowledges thought without judgement.

You are energy. Thought has energy. There is energy power in every thought, word, and action, each having its own particular energy vibration. Whatever course you take in thought, word, or action, that energy vibration is released into the ether, into the outside world. It then is mirrored back to you, in the outside world, for your learning, or others are drawn to you for mutual learning and growth.

Once your thoughts are expressed in words, a double level of energy vibration is created. When those thoughts and words are actioned, the vibration frequency is increase yet again.

It has been established, in particular with Louise Hay and through the science of metaphysics, that most if not all illness is created in the mind. Thoughts send a message to the brain, the brain then responds by sending that thought message out to the body. Just as the body and cells of the body relay messages to the brain, so does the mind affect the body. The mind can even override the messages the cells of the body send to the brain. Many doctors have discovered the power of the brain through research on the power of what is called the placebo effect. Know how powerful you are through the power of your mind. But which mind are you working with? What are you using to think with?

The Three Levels of Consciousness

There are three levels of mind consciousness: your conscious mind, your unconscious or subconscious mind, and your super or higher conscious mind. Each has its own unique role. Understanding each and when each is at work will help you navigate this amazing power within that you have. The subconscious, often referred to as your unconscious mind, is your auto response mind. It has been programmed to be a responder and reacts to various situations or people, much the same as a previous similar situation you've encountered. The conscious mind is the ever-present receptive mind aware of thought, word and deed. It takes in experiences, making them mean something, which is then programmed into the subconscious mind.

The super or higher conscious mind is your creative control centre mind and is directly linked with the greater universal divine source mind. You have access to all three minds at all times, for the mind never sleeps and works all the time. The conscious mind is always taking in information and processing it, and the subconscious accepts the processed information and gives it meaning. Only the higher conscious mind is totally independent of the other minds, being the sole creator of all that is new, without influence of judgement and prejudices.

When awake, you are aware of our conscious mind and conscious of your thoughts, or are you? How often do you seem to drift into an almost-daydream state? How often does your mind wander? This is when you become unconscious, and your subconscious mind takes charge.

As the mind never sleeps; it is never not working, for if it did stop, so would your life. It is your subconscious mind, constantly messaging your brain that ensures all your bodily functions are working. This is done without need for your conscious mind to focus on all that the body has learnt to do automatically. Your heart beats and your blood moves throughout your body, delivering the nutrients each cell needs for survival. The body is a most marvellous machine created by a most amazing mind. The subconscious brain is programmed to send the appropriate messages to the brain so that the body functions in harmony. This same mind level is programmable and has been programmed by you in regard to how you view and respond to any life situation. Just as your body's auto response has been programmed, so too have your emotional and mental responses been programmed. As a human being who has been born with an innate instinct for survival, you have over time programmed your subconscious mind with many levels of fears. These fears are within your subconscious mind; you are mostly unlikely aware of them. However, you often respond automatically to events, people, and situations not from your conscious awareness but rather from your unconscious or subconscious autopilot.

Fear not! For you have a higher conscious mind where inspiration, wisdom, and all you need for your highest good resides. Once you become aware of how the various levels of your mind work, you can become the driver of your fate and the master of your own destiny.

Conscious Mind

You may believe you're consciously aware at all times. This is not always the case. However, when you are fully alert and aware of your thoughts, words, and deeds, you can be confident that you are consciously awake, alert and aware to what you are thinking, saying, and doing in each now moment. When you are working in a conscious state, you are in charge of your mind, the thoughts within your mind, and the decisions you make. You send messages to the brain you wish the brain to respond too. You are consciously programming what you wish the unconscious mind to take on.

From your experiences, you form new thoughts. These then often become your belief systems, and many of these beliefs you conclude to be truth. They then are filed into your subconscious mind so as not to overload your conscious mind, freeing it up to process new experiences. You can choose freely what you wish to believe. This is often referred to as having free will.

The conscious mind is the mind that is in waking awareness. This mind is in awareness to its surroundings, other people, your experiences, and yourself from your perspective. The ideal is to be fully, and at all times, in awareness of all that is in your waking experience, in thought, word, and deed. All too often, it is our unconscious or subconscious mind that is at work, as it is in constant contact with the conscious mind, receiving and storing information from the conscious mind.

You may choose your thoughts, but your life often depends on how powerful your subconscious mind is. Consciously, you may believe all things are possible for you. To determine if that is true, it is vital you check your unconscious thoughts by bringing them into your conscious awareness.

Unconscious or Subconscious Mind

Although most people believe they are always fully conscious when awake they never realise they are often acting unconsciously. This is what is called being on autopilot and being consciously unconscious.

You've all experienced driving somewhere and wondering how you got there, or driving in one direction only to discover that you are not going where you intended but in a direction you often take, even though you needed to go in the opposite direction. Your subconscious autopilot is at work here; you are not being consciously aware until you realise you are not where you need to be. This happens in every aspect of your life. How often do you pay attention to your words, let alone the thoughts that fill your mind? Being physically awake is not always a true indicator that you are consciously aware.

Think of your unconscious mind as the mind that you programmed, for that is what you've done. It is your autopilot brain mind. It is the mind that programmed the body to work in a particular way, automatically, without the need to focus consciously on every breath being taken, every cell working in harmony with every body part. This is the mind, where ego resides, where ego decides what you should believe, feigning free will, where there are only finite possibility thoughts.

The subconscious mind is not an independent thinking mechanism. You operate and navigate your life depending on how it has been programmed. There are great disadvantages if you are not aware of your subconscious programming. You've been programming from the time of birth. Some programming is beneficial to your life, yet others can be harmful. How you perceive and interpret the world around you and how you internalise it becomes your programmed reality.

As the body is controlled by the brain for physical functions, your thoughts control your emotional and mental functions. You usually operate from two emotional modes: love or fear. You have a built-in instinct for survival; over time, humankind has developed an emotional instinct for survival. Just as you respond to any physical threat, you also respond to perceived emotional threats. Where there is no sign of physical danger, the threat is to the emotional mind or the ego self.

Higher or Super Conscious Mind

Your higher conscious mind is the mind that is at one with the divine source mind. In your higher conscious mind, you are at one with all knowledge, wisdom, inspiration, and unconditional love for all. Here you are at one with the will of God, where infinite possibilities are open to you. Here is where you are at one with the creator. Your true creating powers are made possible from this mind space.

This mind transcends the conscious and subconscious mind, for it is the mind at one with the great mind. It is not dictated to, influenced by, or connected to the conscious or subconscious mind. It stands alone, although it speaks to the conscious (and semi-conscious) mind. You have best access to your higher consciousness when in a slightly sleepy state. When in a meditative state, you open yourself up to connecting with your higher consciousness, as well as the great mind of all. It is the connection to this higher self mind where you will access your creativity and where you will create. This great mind is filled with creative thoughts and ideas of greatness accessible to all. This is the place where all the Akashic records reside. Access to these records will open up for you all you need, for all you wish to create, for a joy-filled life.

Have you ever wondered where the great composers, past and present, accessed their musical scores? Where did the wordsmiths find their linguistic masterpieces? How did artists envision things the rest of the world did not see? How did the great inventors discover what no one else did? Through a mind connected to a greater mind for insight and inspiration. You too have access to this great mind. You can choose to connect and discover for yourself the power of your own mind and of the great mind of all.

Individual Ego Self Mind and Your Higher Mind of Spirit

The Internet is one of the most marvellous inventions of our modern times. Have you considered that someone's mind created the Internet? That mind was connected to a great creative force mind, the mind of spirit of its inventor. I love the analogy of the Internet, for it is a great model of connection to the divine source mind and all the individual minds created by this creative mind of all.

Just as there are many individual computers, each is connected to a main power source, having access to all the information on the Internet. So too have you an individual mind that has access to the main frame, the original master source mind. All the knowledge and information you wish to access is available to you: one mind accessing the divine source mind.

If you are not aware of this, you are more likely to access your subconscious ego mind, which only has access to your past thought experiences. It is through your higher conscious mind that you access all experiences, past, present, and future.

Just like a computer, you need to be switched on to access the information you seek from the divine source mind. You can Google the information (so to speak) by asking your higher self and the divine source for the information you seek. If you doubt that it will work, you are likely not to get the information you seek, for you have chosen not to connect. If you don't turn on your computer, you will never be able to access its information. The same thing happens when you believe there is no higher power and there are no possibilities other than what is humanly possible.

Although many people choose not to believe in a higher power, they still believe in their self and their power within. Whatever you choose to believe is your reality. Will you choose that which empowers you or that which holds you back from experiencing joy, happiness, and abundance? Be aware: In this truth, you absolutely have a choice. Your ego mind can be destructive (and it often is). The mind that empowers you is your higher self mind.

Thought Power

Everything you do or say begins with a thought. Pay attention to your thoughts and where they are coming from. Is it from ego or your higher self? Do you know (or are you even aware of) the many thoughts in your mind? In knowing your true thoughts, pay attention to your words. They are the indicators of your thoughts. You may have experienced saying something you never meant to say. If so, be aware that the first words out of your mouth are part of your unconscious thought system. If you don't consciously agree with what you've just said, that is a thought you need to let go of; change it and replace it with your new conscious mindset. Don't just ignore it. Replace it, for you will find yourself in autopilot regarding a thought you no longer agree with (perhaps never agreed with).

Consider how often you approach a person or situation from a level of fear, a fear often based on a past experience; you may be fearful of the same negative experience. And then you are often proven to be right. You have not attracted that to you. You've just recreated that programmed experience into your unconscious mind, replaying the experience. You are in unconscious awareness, rather than consciously responding to this new situation or person in now time. You are effectively recreating the past, a past you believe (often unconsciously) to be the only possible outcome within an experience you believe to be the same. You are not allowing for the possibility for change and the reality of changing experiences and growth in others or yourself.

Particularly upsetting (or even traumatic) are the negative impacting events in your childhood that seem to have dominance over happy memories. Do you wonder why your negative thoughts or memories sometimes dominate your thoughts? Why do you think it is so? Or do you even consider this fact? Why is it that these past memories are still impacting your now life experience? Is the answer simple? Is it complex? Or is there an answer at all? What if yes is the answer to all three questions? What if that answers is no to all three? What if the answer is both yes and no?

I always ask the higher source mind within me for any answer I seek. I seek to understand why we hold on to past negative experience memories, emotionally impacting the present now experience. The answer seems simple, at first, yet I can see where it can be complex on another level.

The answer is, you get to choose your thoughts, what you wish or want to remember. Life experiences are just that: experiences. If you have not been able to move past the past or to let go of it, you still have something to learn from it. It may be that it is about forgiveness: forgiveness for another or yourself. Forgiveness is not about condoning an action or behaviour. It is the recognition of another spirit who for whatever reason has no cognition of the impact their actions or behaviour on another and their self. I am reminded of the words of Christ: "Forgive them, Lord, for they know not what they do." And in that context, forgiveness is given, and you are released from the past. Sometimes, it is about releasing yourself from past blame, shame, or judgement as you forgive yourself, for had you known better, you would have done better.

Now choose your memories. I can almost hear you saying that a negative memory that is traumatic can only be a traumatic memory. I am not telling you not to recognise the level of the experience on the scale of good or bad, pleasurable or painful. Rather, which memories would you rather focus on? Perhaps you need to focus on the painful. Perhaps you need to heal that pain. How do you measure your healing if not by moving on from that unhappy memory? Leave it where it belongs: in the past. Choose to focus on happiness and happiness memories? If you have no happy memories, choose to be happy now for your future to contain happy memories.

Perception

"In the sky, there is no distinction of east and west.

People create distinctions out of their own minds

and then believe them to be true."

—Buddha

My first experience of perceptions, other than my own, was in my later years as a primary teacher. Call me naïve, and I certainly was regarding other ways of being and seeing. I clearly remember (or was my mind impregnated with a thought from a greater mind intelligence?) coming out of a staff meeting and hearing others say what they heard. I was amazed that I had not heard what they had. I was certain they hadn't heard correctly, and I was perplexed. How could we all be at the same meeting, hearing the same words spoken, and have such varying recollections of what was said? I had no answer. I couldn't understand. It was not until years later, in my metaphysical studies, that I came to understand the concept of different perceptions. I came to truly understand the nature of seeing, hearing, and interpreting. I could see that each of us is different physically. However, what I couldn't see was the mind. I couldn't relate to the difference in interpretations and of different perceptions, for I hadn't understood these differences or how they come about.

What is perception but a way of understanding and interpreting what you see, hear, or feel about life, the world, and the people therein? When you perceive, you put a meaning to what you see, and from there, you make a judgement or put a value to the situation, event, or person. You gain impressions and interpret these impressions, conceptualising them to understand what you believe you are seeing, feeling, and experiencing. What you don't realise is that you often put a meaning to something due to your unconscious thought systems.

There are so many things that influence your perception, for perception first begins in the mind. You are influenced by so many things that affect your perception. You begin as a child of parents who view the world, their life, and the environment in a particular way. That perception is taught to you though your experiences with your parents. You are taught what things mean, not only in the physical world but your mental and emotional world. You learn to have certain beliefs, prejudices, and values, and you also learn to make judgements. As a child, you may have been very sensitive in picking up on the emotional state of the energy vibration of others. Over time, it can unknowingly become your own vibration. As you grow older and mix with siblings and friends, you became influenced by their interpretation and view of the world, as they did with yours. Your heritage, culture, religious background, social groups, and society in general all have a profound impact on how you choose to view the world. I say "choose," for you do so, whether it is consciously or unconsciously.

Perception can also be likened to a mirage. You are seeing from a place of past information, being delusional, seeing a false now world rather than reality. You are parched, thirsty for truth; in world devoid of truth, your mind wanders, believing to see something that is not there. This past is recreated?: "I am not good enough," "all people who are not white are inferior," "men are physically stronger than women so they must be stronger mentally too." These may not be your beliefs, but they are reality for many people.

Shared Perception or Not

You might presume that because everyone is in agreement that a particular object is a chair or a tree (or a person is a man or woman), that everything is interpreted similarly. So any situation or event of human interaction is thought to be interpreted similarly. But no and know!

Know that you cannot perceive like another, for you do not think the same and have not had the same experiences (even though some may seem similar). Why is it that in a family of many children, each will recount their childhood experiences differently? Perception! It's all about personal meaning interpretation; each is valid for the person perceiving for their individual learning and wisdom growth.

You just have to ask someone what they see when looking at a picture you are also viewing, to know they have their own focus, which is not the same as yours. Is this wrong? Of course not! It is just different, like as the features of their face are different compared to yours, for within their mind are different thoughts around what they see and what they experience. You may not agree with or like someone else's viewpoint, nor do you have to. Just know they view the world differently and can't understand multidimensional thinking; this is not your responsibility. Nor can you change their mind. Only they can. That will always be their right of choice, as you have that right too. You can only be responsible for yourself: what you think, say, and do. Picture a view of a mountain, a lake, or the ocean. What do you see? How does the view move you? What do you feel when you take in the view? Where would your sensory memories go? Is your opinion of the view positive or negative? If someone else looked at the same view, would they see, think, feel, or remember the view exactly the same way as you?

It is highly unlikely that the both of you will interpret the shared vision exactly the same way. And that is due to so many variables. Even so, many people believe we should think alike and have the same values, beliefs, judgements, and ethics. Although no one has the exact same experience as another, somehow many people believe the end resultant understanding of shared life experiences should be the same. Perhaps a new or better understanding of differing human perception will bring with it tolerance and compassion.

Multidimensional Thinking

A coin has two sides. All too often, people focus on only one side of any point, idea, or argument. Few people acknowledge, recognise, or are willing to see another point of view. The universe and all within it is multidimensional, with multiple ways of looking, seeing, and interpreting a situation, event, or person. This multidimensional universe is often referred to as the Matrix. Within the matrix are many possible realities. In other words, there are many and various points of view, and each is the reality of the person who perceives it. Each of us sees and believes in only one dimension: our own viewpoint or opinion. Being aware of another's point of view opens you up to their reality. I call this the second dimension and second-dimensional thinking. When you are aware that everyone has their own version of reality, you allow yourself to be open to what I call multidimensional thinking.

When working with my clients regarding perception, I refer to the many levels of perception as dimensional thinking: one dimensional, two dimensional, three dimensional, or multidimensional. Most people are one-dimensional thinkers; they do so for many years (some for all their lifetime). Two-dimensional thinking is when you accept that others think differently from you. Three-dimensional thinking is the recognition that yet another perspective is also possible: another way of thinking and another way of interpreting the same situation, event, or person. Multidimensional thinking recognises that many people exist, have existed, and will exist in the world; there are differing perceptions and differing interpretations to life and life experiences. This understanding is the first step in true acceptance, tolerance, and compassion of self and another.

As a multidimensional thinker, you are aware and know that there are many ways of looking at life and your experiences. At the same time, you know others see life in their own unique way. You then become more tolerant and respectful to other ways of thinking and being. In fact, who are you not to? If you lack tolerance or respect for another's point of view, whether you agree with it or not, you are the one to experience discomfort in your life, for it is your mind that is disturbed, your mind that is uneasy. It is impossible to be happy and joyful when you don't have peace of mind.

No two people perceive the same way. It is not possible, as no two people, even siblings, share exactly the same experience, past or present. Therefore, no two people can fully understand the way each other perceives reality. And no one vision of reality is better than another's, other than in judgement. Being at peace with others having a different understanding of the world will help you. Expecting others to think, feel, see, and like you often leads to disappointment and disillusionment. How often do you find it difficult to agree with another's opinion, belief, or view of the world? We all want our views, opinions, and beliefs validated by others. Yet we can fail to recognise the uniqueness, not only in ourselves but in others. Learning acceptance and tolerance of others and the difference within yourself will ease the burden of expectation you most often put on yourself.

To believe your perception is the only one is not a truth but an illusion. The reality is that we all think, feel, and experience life uniquely from our point of view, through the individual experiences we have had. Each of us interprets those experiences and what meaning we give them as our own. These factors influence your perception of life for your future experiences.

What is reality but only the perception of it? You've created reality in your mind. The good news is, you can change your created reality if you need it to be different.

A painter can paint over a canvas with another look or choose a fresh new canvas to paint on. Consider this: Are you painting the same picture over and over again, trying to make it look better, adding details you thought you missed? This is fine, if that's what you want to do and what you believe will make your life better. Consider also you can have a new canvas, a new mindset to begin anew, to create the new artwork of your life.

A new thought will create a new reality. You just need to learn to change your mind about your mind. Which mind will you work with? Which mind will attract what you want?

Free Will: The Power of Choice

We all have free will, which is but the power of choice. Once you recognise this wonderful gift, you are more likely to use this gift for your benefit. I say it is a gift, for the divine source, the creator of all, gave all of humankind this gift.

Many people believe they don't have a choice. Some people do not have the same freedoms enjoyed by those in the Western world. However, I speak now of freedom within your own mind. Nelson Mandela is evidence of someone who, although imprisoned physically for many years, never gave up the freedom of his mind. And he was able to survive where others would not have, for he did not allow his mind to be imprisoned. Your mind is no less free; it is only imprisoned if you allow it to be. You are free to think, feel, and act as you wish.

In understanding the law of cause and effect, know that whatever you choose to think, feel, or do will affect you in some way or another.

How do you wish to be? What effect do you wish to experience in your life? Think about it. Think about the possible outcomes when you speak or act in a particular way. Will it have a positive, empowering effect for you? You have no control on how it affects others, only on yourself. However, if the effect on others also affects you, take that into consideration. You are the cause of your experience. You are in charge of what you think, say, and do. You are also in charge of how you are affected by what others say and do in regard to you and your shared experience with them. Don't think you don't have the power of choice when interacting with others. You can choose how you will be impacted by what is said or done in your shared experience.

Sometimes, you may believe you are choosing, but you've been brainwashed, almost hypnotised, to make a choice that may not be your will. Advertising and clever marketing is a prime example of how your will, your choosing, can be manipulate.

The world can be a playground or a war zone. What do you see? Which do you want? You may think that you don't have a choice, that everything is as it is because that's just how life is. You see evidence of wars going on in the world and even perhaps in your own life. People are suffering and dealing with physical, emotional, and mental pain and anguish. Most people would say if they had a choice, they wouldn't choose their situation. An event isn't always a choice. How it's dealt with is where choice is available to you. Do you choose defeat or victory? Do you see yourself as victim or visionary? Do you allow a situation, event, or person to define you, or are you the creator of your own self and your life? The choice is yours to make, and in each moment, you make it. Make it from now on in full awareness. Choose your thoughts, your power, and your creative abilities, if only to see life and experience it differently if you have not yet chosen *you*.

Mind Health

Having a healthy mind is not only as important as having physical wellness but even more so, because mental health impacts your physical well-being. You know what makes for physical fitness, which leads to physical wellness. Eating well, exercising, and even correcting any chemical imbalances all lead to physical well-being. Mental and emotional well-being also impact your physical health. Just as the body needs good food and exercise to maintain it at optimum health, so too does the mind need thought nourishment and mental movement. Have you ever heard someone say, "That is food for thought"? Well, what food are you giving your mind through your foods of thought, fear, or love? Exercise your thoughts through your conscious awareness. Are you working with your conscious mind to connect with your higher self mind to work on that higher plane? Or are you on autopilot, allowing the subconscious mind to do the work for you?

Be mindful and fill your mind with wonderfully empowering thoughts. Say positive affirmations and believe them. Meditate regularly so as to connect with your higher God mind.

Channelled Insight

In the deep recesses of your mind lies all the wisdom and inspiration you need for all your lifetimes: lifetimes of learning, of knowledge, of growth.

Each experience has brought you closer to the truth, brought you closer to the truth of you, one in which your greatness resides.

The mind your mind is at one with is the great mind of all, a mind loving and knowing the loving creations of its mind.

All you need to know now is that your mind is your greatest asset here in your experience. Use it wisely.

Don't compromise. Don't avoid.

Experience in joy, the joy of the power of your mind.

Affirmation Statements

- I am at one with my higher conscious mind.

- I allow thoughts of joy, happiness, and love into my mind now.

- I know that my mind creates and am connected to it now.

- I am aware of the power of my mind.

- I choose to now work for my highest good in all things and in all ways.

- In awareness, I change my thoughts of fear to thoughts of love.

Follow-Up Tasks

- Learn to change your mind about your mind.

- Take time out each day to meditate.

- Pay attention to your thoughts.

- Pay attention to your words.

- Be willing to change your thought and words, particularly if you don't agree with them.

CHAPTER 7

The Law of Creation

The Power to Be

"Creation is the calling into existence of that which
does not exist in the objective world."

—Charles F. Haanel

Oxford Dictionary

Create 1. Bring into existence, cause, 2. originate.

Creation 1. Creating or being created, 2. God's creating of the
universe.

Law Definition

Making something out of nothingness, through thought power and
being at one with the divine source.

In the Beginning

Whether you believe the world was created in seven days, in a moment, or due to a Big Bang, the consensus seems to be it was created and created out of nothing (no matter). There certainly is evidence that the world exists, for it is said, "Seeing is believing." This world evidence is in the physical reality: the land, the sky, the creatures large and small, the waterways, and the human beings who inhabit this planet. Each in itself is a wonderful and wondrous creation. When you take time to dwell on each creation, say a bird, a flower, a tree, or your own physical anatomy, your body, each is a marvel in itself. Who is the cause or the creator of these end resultant creations? Some will say Mother Nature; others call this creator Father God. Scientists would have you believe that unseeable molecules, atoms, protons, and neutrons are the cause. Some others believe a mind greater than all minds combined created all you see. Others believe it to be an alien race. People of faith say a being they call God was the creator of your life and your physical reality.

From the earliest recorded history of humankind, there has always been belief in a power source greater than the human self. This source is often called God. Many different names have been given to this source: universal life force, God mind, universal energy, or as I like to say, the source of all: divine source love. Whatever you wish to believe is your right of free will. Suffice to say, I do believe in a power source greater than my own and greater than the sum total of all. That is the source of all power, and I plug into it when I choose to learn, grow, or create beyond my human self. The mind that is the creator of all is greater than the individual human mind. The human mind cannot conceive the power of the great mind it is connected to. Although billions of bits of information, resulting in myriad thoughts, may enter your brain, it can only process a few thousand. Yet when you are paying attention to your thoughts, what mind is doing the noticing of your thoughts within your mind?

Beyond the laws of the universe resides a spirit of creation, creating by extending out in love, manifesting its thoughts into physical reality. You are but a mirror reflection of that vision extension. By extending yourself in love, you are able to understand in some small way what is happening and how your universe and all that it entails is ever evolving, further creating and being created. You are but another part of this creator, also creating because you are able to. You see the ever creating abilities of nature, the animal kingdom, and humankind itself, the never-ending cycle of creation and recreation. You are also a creator, ever creating in awareness or making the unreal real in unawareness.

Few people are aware of their own power to create. It is not until their outlook on the world is distressing them that they seek to better understand others and themselves. Often, this is when the journey back to their self begins. They come looking for answers to life questions, in particular about their role in the world and this life experience. They may be looking to build their self-confidence, as they are dissatisfied with their life. They may be needing help with an event that is troubling them and which they are unable to deal effectively with. They may be experiencing family conflict or issues with work colleagues or their boss. Everyone on some level is searching to find a meaning to their life. For some, a meaning to life no long seems to exist. Some give up, believing there is no meaning or a meaning cannot be found. Others, like yourself, go in search for the meaning. Within themselves, they know there is something to be found that has been lost.

The Creator Mind

Your higher self mind is the centre of your creative abilities. Your mind is thinking every second, every minute, and every hour. Every thought that passes is rich in possibilities yet to be manifested. What if I told you all of them are manifest? Billions of people exist with billions of thoughts floating around in the ether. Be not surprised, then, at the many and various actions and attractions that are yours in physical reality. Thoughts of love, of war, of fear, of fright, of flight and fight all float though the fabric of your universe.

The mind is a powerhouse of making and creating. Here, I make a distinction between things that are made and things that are created by you. Your mind is constantly making what you decide to give energy thought to. It is also able to create. You make in every moment of your thinking life. You create when you are at one in awareness with the divine source, the true creator of all. When your mind is one with the divine source mind, which mind is manifesting and what? Ego mind makes from thoughts of fear and lack. God mind creates from a place of unconditional love all that is new and unique, with the mind choosing to create in unison with divine source mind.

In human form, you have two minds (although in truth you have but one). The mind that thinks it is only human is the ego mind. Ego was made up by you through your power, your free will, and your connection with infinite intelligence. Ego cannot create. Ego can, however, manifest into your deluded reality that which you believe in. You've told ego what to make. It is a made-up part of you, but not the spirit of who you truly are. Ego makes true what you fear. Ego was not born of love; it grew out of your fears. If ego was all you truly are, then the world would not have love, joy, or happiness. Fear would have a stronghold.

Your creations begin with your visions. When you begin with your vision and then go on to use your creative abilities and the creative processes, you bring into manifestation your vision for your reality. Your make this happen when you do it in a loving space, with integrity and from the place of truth. Then and only then does the universe work with you, using divine timing and purpose to deliver your request, in this time space reality.

Know that when you create, you do not create alone. It is only with the divine source where creation is truly manifest. Consider a wonderful piece of music, a powerful story, some artwork that moves or inspires. They were all created in a place of love or passion, driven by a source within that seems beyond the human condition.

Creative Thought and Creating

You've been given the ability to create from your creator. However, as you came into a world in unawareness, not knowing who you truly are, fear of this new world was instilled in your human nature. Yet the call of your true nature could not go unheard, and in time, the need to come into awareness took hold. Those who are in awareness are charged with the responsibility to awaken those still asleep.

So awaken, dear dreamer, to the reality of your creator and your ability to create. Make no longer the unreal real.

Create what you were created to be. Create what only you know how to.

Create in the vibration of love, and your creations will last eternity.

On your life journey, you can follow another's experiences or create your own unique life. That may take trial and error, as you uncover what you wish to achieve and how. Begin with a desire for the life you wish to lead. Then you may try different experiences, as each will give you insights on your road to achieve your desires. You will come to realise that some things lead you closer to your desired outcome, while others don't. Know that this only happens when you are creating in awareness and consciously pay attention to your thoughts, words, and actions.

The desire is to create something unique and to reflect the individuality of the creator; creating is within us all. When you are working in the space of pure love and passion drives you (or you feel driven by it), this is often explained as, "Your creative juices are flowing."

You may have forgotten you're here to experience a physical existence and manifest from your spirit mind, creating uniquely that which is specific to yourself. You are a special piece in the tapestry of life, in the jigsaw puzzle of the universe. No two are alike, and no two have the same purpose. You have evidence, I know, of those who have made a profound difference in the world, those who have left a legacy of some wonderful inspirational deed, be it in word, picture, song, invention, or action. Did they set out to create a legacy or just fulfil their need to create? Yet it is their creation that you are blessed to know.

You are a profound creation also. You are creating a legacy of your own, and it impacts each of us in some way or another. Most importantly, it impacts you and who you are. Choose to know who you are, who you choose to be, and who you wish to become. You have the power to create yourself to be the best version of the created you in human form. Or you can continue to recreate a past illusionary version of yourself. Now that you are in awareness of what you do and are capable of doing, choose, for you can. Know also that in not choosing, you choose. As true creators who have been capable of bringing into existence what wasn't true, you can create truth anew.

Cocreation

It has been recorded, perhaps, but not fully realised that many people over the centuries have created in full awareness of the creator and the ability to manifest wonders by cocreating with the Divine Source Intelligence, the creator of all. What would our world, your life, and you look like if you chose to cocreate with the divine? Just imagine what your life experiences would be. Is it possible for everyone to experience heaven on earth, rather than only a few being able to recognise that reality? This is what I believe we are all moving towards, even though it may seem that chaos reigns in some corners of the world. I know the acorn that becomes the oak tree must be broken for it to grow. So too, it seems, humankind must struggle with false beliefs and the false illusions of the ego for growth. These, then, will be broken down, broken apart for the beauty within to be revealed and to grow into their full potential. This is happening all over the world within individuals. Each will help others, who perhaps are having trouble breaking through. Sometimes, growth needs help, for as one connects with their joy and true purpose, others will follow. As that vibrational energy grows stronger, it magnetises others towards their own evolution and with their own creation unearthed.

Knowing that you created the ego self from a power base of the spirit of who you are is enlightening. Finally, you recognise the strength of your ego. You now have evidence of the strength of you. All that is needed now is to override the false ego and embrace the true you and the true power of you. Knowing that this power is at your disposal (and in truth is your true nature, in spirit) can be disconcerting, as much as it is enlightening. It is therefore important that you don't make yourself wrong for not realising it sooner. Be joyful that you have come to realise it now, knowing that everything is working perfectly and in perfect harmony with divine timing.

Let go and let the God mind be the cause of your life and what you would like to achieve therein. I am sure you've heard of the saying "Let go, let God." People don't always know what that means or how to do it. If you are not sure what you want or need or are fearful of not being able to be aligned to get what you want, give your fears and doubts to the divine source. Release them into the ether for the divine source to heal and reveal all to you.

Just say, "I don't know what to do. I don't know how to handle this situation. I need your divine help or insight. I give it up to you; I release my worries, fears, and doubts into your care. May your wisdom regarding this situation be revealed to me for my understanding. Thank you for taking care of this for me."

The divine source, as your creator, like any loving parent, wants to give you all the world has to offer. You so often humbly decline, saying, "I am not worthy," or "I don't deserve this." So the divine source says, "I won't force this on you. It is here for you, my darling creation, anytime you are ready to have the gifts I offer. Abundance in all things of joy, especially love." When you are ready to accept the gifts on offer from the divine source, they are there but for the asking. Loving acceptance is the key.

Creation or Recreation

Do you know the difference between creating and recreating? Or is it not one and the same?

Creation, as stated in the beginning of this chapter, is bringing into existence or causing something to be. Recreation is creating, over and over again, the past, bringing into existence a situation that seems similar. Have you not experienced this to be so? You may do so unknowingly, unconsciously. Why do you recreate? Is there value in recreation, and if so, what is the value?

You may have had an unhappy experience with a person, and years later, you come across someone else with a similar personality. You may then have a similar experience with them. It may seem as if you have attracted that to yourself, yet the power of you has recreated the situation, event, or experience for a variety of reasons. You may be aware of a situation that you seem to be reliving, or you may be in unawareness. Consciously, you are not likely to want to recreate any experiences that caused you distress on any level. There are various reasons recreation occurs; it occurs more often than creation. It may be because you have some unfinished business regarding the person, even though they may not be exactly alike. You may need to learn something missed in the last experience. Or perhaps you would have liked to have handled it differently, and you are now given the opportunity to do so.

You may experience these recreated moments years after a similar experience. You now have a different perspective, a better understanding, and more knowledge. You now have the opportunity to create and be the cause for a different outcome, a different effect. You may not succeed in having a different outcome. However, you have the opportunity to make a difference, and with each experience, you learn something new. The learning can be positive or negative; you can choose which you wish to focus on. Remember that you are a powerful creative force. Choose how you wish to use your power. What you are going to use your energy for: creation or recreation?

You are a creative being having a human experience. So the human experience needs to be honoured before the human self is ready, willing, and able to connect with your higher spiritual self. It must go on a journey of self-discovery for self-awareness: awareness of what it is, truly, to be human. The human being has physical needs, these being shelter, food, water, sleep, security, and love. Over the course of your lifetime, you have many experiences, each teaching you more about yourself, others, and the world you are experiencing. Your creative nature looks to discover what it is you wish to create. You seek to find your purpose, your reason to be.

Yet the human experience seems to bring into being a different creative process: that of recreation rather than creation. You recreate situations and draw people into your life over and over again. Each situation or event may seem different yet will have similarities to other situations and events. The people you have issues with may appear in your life in different forms, yet the issues seem to be repeated. Everything is recreation rather than creation.

Rather than attracting a situation or person, you unconsciously recreate the scenario for your learning and growth. Seek to gain a better understanding of each recreated experience. What you believe, which is the cause of things that unfold, and what you passionately want are all in play for any repeat experience unfolding. Often, it is also done in partnership with spirit and the universe. Divine source love is ever ready and at hand to help, guide, and support your human journey.

You often recreate in unawareness. When you hear the concept of "Live in the now," you are encouraged to leave the past where it happened: in the past. Reminding yourself of (or reliving) past experiences ensures you will continue to recreate these or similar experiences in the future, effectively making them your now experience. Then you are only recreating situations and meeting people who are a mirror image of that past you are holding onto. You have forgotten that it has passed and is no longer your reality. You are only keeping the illusion alive. This you do from the power of creation you possess. Once you realise what you are doing, learn from it so you can move into the present now moment. What would you choose: to recreate past pains or create new gains? The choice is yours.

Take back control through the power of your God mind by reconnecting with who you truly are: a loving being, not the ego mind of fear and illusion. All great creations were born out of love, not fear. Those who believe fear needs to be the motivator have never known, experienced or given credit to the motivator that is passion born out of love.

In human form, you can only recreate. But in spirit, you cocreate with the divine source. You can do this freely, and you can do it with the help, support, and guidance of the divine source. You also have constant help and support from your angels and guides. They are appointed by the divine source to be ever at your side, whenever you are in need or wish to call upon them. Be aware: They are not permitted to interfere with your free will and can only help when requested.

They are ever present and ever available; you just have to ask ... and you will receive.

Power to Create

Listen to the voice in your head: the one that is constructive, not destructive, the voice of love, not the voice of fear. You have been listening to the voice of ego for so long that you may not be able to hear the voice of love too clearly at first. The voice will be quiet, for ego is loud and brash. The voice of love may be quiet, but it is patient and persistent, waiting for you to hear the truth. The voice will remind you of who you truly are, what your true purpose is, and how much you are loved: how fully you are at one with love. In that vibration of loving acceptance of this human journey, you will discover everything is just as it's meant to be, for the highest good of all. You will come to realise when human ego is in play and where the hand of God is at work. You are at all times being looked after, perfectly. You will only realise this as you move from the illusions you have recreated to the reality of the human journey and the spiritual significance that is beyond the physical experience. When you are at one with the great universal mind, you will create all you desire to experience, in joy, happiness, and love. Perhaps you are already doing this without awareness, aware only of what is passionately driving you.

Visualise or imagine for your creation process to begin. Believe in that which you want to create: your desired reality. Believe it is possible for you. Imagine yourself having all you desire. Know that what you desire will not interfere with another's right of free will. Trust the universe to send to you people, signs, and situations to support your manifestation. Then be ever alert and ready to take action when these come to be. Also be aware that God works to divine timing, rather than any human clockwork. Patience along with trust are the two key spiritual learning curves throughout this creative process.

All Is Created

You are constantly creating (or recreating). The world you see around you is the one you have created (or recreated) for yourself. You also get to see the worlds others have created (or recreated) for themselves. Your ego mind recreates your world of illusion. Your God mind is your creative force mind.

You are the physical manifestation of spirit (God/the universal energy/the divine source mind/the all). You are having the human experience of and for spirit.

When connected with spirit and with your own true spiritual nature, you are able to create beyond your wildest imaginings, for you are not creating alone. You are creating in partnership with spirit. And together, in partnership, is where I believe miracles happen.

However, you are the tool (so to speak) that is able to act on and have the experience of spirit's vision (thoughts). You get guidance for your desires and your visions to become your reality. You need to be in a state of awareness to recognise this help. You will then know when to take action on the road to manifesting your visions.

Know also you have free will, and spirit will not interfere or dictate your will to you. The choices of your life and how to live it are yours. You can do whatever you will with this life experience, although you can also choose to seek help from spirit connecting with your higher self, the spirit of you, for a better life experience.

It is important to know that nothing you wish to create for yourself or your life can be in conflict with another. People have their own power, creative urges, and free will. Everyone is allowed to choose for themselves but not for another. It is for others to choose and create for themselves.

What do you choose to create in and for your life?

Work in and with spirit in your working life, in your everyday life.

Channelled Insight

When did you create alone, dear child? Never.

We are as one, and together we create.

We create your choosing in the knowing that everything is for your highest good.

I liken you to me and me to you.

You are my hands, feet, and body.

I am ever at your side.

I know what you know and do what you will.

You are my apprentice.

I am ever masterful.

For you are my greatest masterpiece.

Know this: Be not afraid.

Abide in love.

Creation is my offer to you.

You are my gift to me.

Affirmation Statements

- I create in awareness.

- I am a creative being with creative powers.

- I create now.

- I am in alignment mentally, emotionally, and in reality with that which I choose to create.

- I am a powerful, loving being.

- I am creating the life of my choosing.

- I choose to create _____ in my life (for my life).

- I choose to experience _____.

Follow-Up Tasks

- Meditate regularly. Take the time to learn how to meditate. Begin by meditating for just a few minutes and build up to at least fifteen minutes each day.

- Pray for creative insight and inspiration. There is great power in prayer.

- Visualise that which you have chosen to create.

- Feel the emotional joy and happiness that you believe you will experience once your creation is manifest. Doing so will put you in vibrational alignment with what you wish to attract.

- Believe. Believe you have in a future now what you wish to create or attract.

- Be in the knowing. Know that you have already that which you wish to attract.

CHAPTER 8

Conclusion

We, as humans, are complex beings physically, emotionally, and mentally. Numberless thoughts enter our mind in any given moment. The way we process them varies with each individual. People view the world from their own unique perspective. There are many variables that influence thoughts, including our thoughts about ourselves. Many of our thoughts become beliefs that lead to other thoughts related to our belief systems. Our beliefs are formed through our perception, our translation, of the world around us. Translating what we see into our language means that what we see is coming from our perspective. Often, translations cannot be fully and accurately matched from one perspective to another, and inaccuracies and misunderstandings occur. It is also important to note that much of what we accept was imposed upon us. These imposed sources are many and varied. Yet we rarely, if ever, revisit our beliefs to acknowledge them and to test their validity in determining if they are relevant (or in fact ever were). The notions we hold about ourselves are usually the last ones we would question. The reasons for this include fear and self-doubt, all due to thoughts and views that sabotage the self.

We trust in the wisdom of others, of organisations, and of society as a whole, not aware that we may be denying our own wisdom. What is considered to be true by one may not be assumed by another. Take, for example, if one's expertise is in teaching, while another's is in information technology; does this mean one person is better than another? We often make personal judgements based on limited facts. It is a choice that each mind has made and maintains to be true. There are positive beliefs in the self which enhance self-belief. When the belief is "I can't teach" or "I am no good at modern technology," these thoughts can lead to lower self-esteem, thus impacting on self-belief. The power in self-belief makes all things possible to the self, within the knowledge of the God self.

Once that truth is established, then self-belief cannot waver.

Knowing the God self and knowing that all-encompassing power energy is knowledge of the truth of who you are. In recognising this truth, you can no longer accept falsehoods and illusions of a limited self. However, not everyone is ready to acknowledge this aspect of their nature.

As our human needs are met physically (food, shelter, safety) and emotionally (love, acceptance), we begin to look to meet our need for self-actualisation. This is our highest need, our connection to our spiritual self. We begin to recognise that although our physical needs may be met, we are still somehow unsatisfied. We feel that life is not what we thought it would be. And some people feel this, even though they have a nice home, material goods, and plenty of food. Even if emotional needs have been met, through the loving people around us (partners, family, and friends), something may seem to be missing, and life may still be filled with distress. What is missing, perhaps, is self-love and self-acceptance. We alone can fulfil that need through self-belief.

Modern society and the conscious collective exert a significant impact on our self-esteem and self-concept. Society has a multitude of sayings and proverbs which people begin to accept as true. Many of them are self-defeating. "Nobody is perfect" keeps us believing that perfection, whatever that is, is unattainable (although it gives many a sense of relief that they do not have to achieve the unrealistic expectations of others). Often, it is the catalyst for others to beat themselves up, believing that whatever they do or achieve is never enough, for it is not perfect. Blonde and Irish jokes insinuate that all blondes and all Irish are dumb. Although the jokes may be funny, some begin to imagine that this is true. They then begin to perceive these people as dumb (or if they are blonde or Irish, they begin to believe in this stereotyping).

The saying, "A woman's place is in the home" came from a belief that women were only meant to stay at home and look after the family. "What you don't know won't hurt you" gives you the impression that a lack of knowledge is better than knowing the truth. Some sayings and proverbs give us life experience insights which are positive. However, those that give a negative impression invalidate our sense of self. It is our interpretation that dictates the level of self-belief. However, a mindset that looks to enhance its belief in life and self energises self-belief.

You can use visualisation to attract to you what you want.

As you focus on what you want, being in that vibrational alignment will attract it to you.

You are now aware of the reality of the law of cause and effect. There is a cause for everything that happens in your life. So you can now work to discover where the cause is in any particular effect on you in your life. If it began with you, work to discover how you can change your thoughts, words, or actions, to change your life for the better. If it began with another, the cause is for them to work on to change, if they so choose.

Knowing the power in the law of belief, you can begin checking your belief systems around that which you desire. This will help you know if your vibration is in alignment with your desire or not. Are you blocking your wants and desires? If so, why, and how can you change your belief thoughts to align with what you choose to attract into your life to experience? Then decide which beliefs are true and therefore worthy of keeping, along with those you need to let go of. Once in alignment, pay attention to the signs from the universe for when to take the right action to make your dreams come true.

Finally, look at whether you are loving (or not) that which you want in your life.

The law of love transcends all the others and works always for your highest good. Loving and accepting each manifested creation unconditionally will free you from seeing fault, seeing fear, seeing error, and making judgements; it will open you up to see the truth.

Acknowledge the missed understanding and missed interpretations of your previous perceptions. Trust in yourself and the powerful knowledge that is your heritage, your lineage, and divine in nature.

You are the manifested thought form of the divine source of all.

You now have the knowledge of your true nature. You now are aware of your true worth and value. You have every reason to possess a strong sense of yourself and true self-belief. Awakening to this realisation is crucial. Your self-belief resides in this knowledge. With this knowledge, there can be no doubt as to your self-worth. There is no longer a reason to sabotage yourself or to have low self-esteem, for now, you know your divinity.

For too long, you have fortified the evidence to the contrary, reinforcing what you believed and accepted to be true about yourself. You thought you were only human, all the while not knowing your divine nature. Recognising your connection to the universal oneness begins your understanding and the return to your true self. How you process all this information and begin to renew your thoughts and beliefs about yourself is the next stage towards self-mastery. That which you believe positively empowers you for self-belief, gaining you self-mastery. What beliefs are worthy of retaining other than the truth? Sometimes, people cling to their fears and illusions as to a friendship that's run its cause. Something they have had for so long seems to feel safe. All the while, they are unaware of the destructive impact it is having on their life and their self.

Believing in yourself through the knowledge of your creator God, the divine source love, is the most powerful understanding of who you truly are. Knowing the truth of who you are ascertains your true essence and nature. Having faith and belief in this self, the God self, is the most powerful evidence for your own self-belief.

In each generation, and over many centuries, elders, mystics, prophets, and intuitives have been the gatekeepers of eternal knowledge. They pass down the mysteries of the universe and its laws through word, song, and story. It is written in every folklore, fairy tale, and fable. It is spoken and written in every spiritual book. As once the seeds of knowledge were written in the wind, so now they are in every vibration, in every cell of energy, for each of us to attune to and align with the knowledge. Play no more just one note for the song of your soul. Know the full scale of notes available for your soul to sing.

As before is now.

What once was not seen is seen once more.

What was once not known is known again.

Nurture your seeds of knowledge. Add my insight into the array of knowledge you so far have gained, creating your own book of knowledge.

I set my mind at rest, knowing others now can follow when the body is laid to rest to play in peace and joyful understanding that everything is as it is and as it should be, until we beings all once more just be ... who we truly are.

And the story continues. How shall it be? What will you make it be? Then so it shall be.

And so it is.

Printed in the United States
By Bookmasters